Take-Home Leveled Readers

Advanced Level

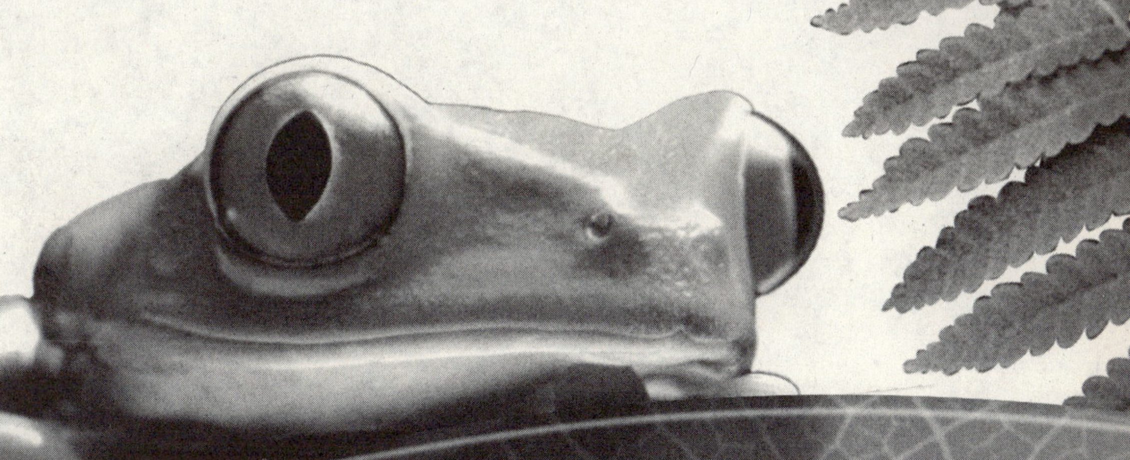

Science

PEARSON

Scott Foresman

Editorial Offices: Glenview, Illinois • Parsippany, New Jersey • New York, New York
Sales Ofices: Needham, Massachusetts • Duluth, Georgia • Glenview, Illinois
Coppell, Texas • Sacramento, California • Mesa, Arizona

sfsuccessnet.com

ISBN: 0-328-19723-8

2 3 4 5 6 7 8 9 10 V004 13 12 11 10 09 08 07 06 05

Table of Contents

Chapter 1	Desert Plants	1–14
Chapter 2	Nocturnal Animals	15–28
Chapter 3	Life in a Rain Forest	29–42
Chapter 4	Animal Eggs	43–56
Chapter 5	Crystals and Gems	57–70
Chapter 6	How Clouds Are Made	71–84
Chapter 7	Tyrannosaurus rex	85–94
Chapter 8	Air Is Everywhere	95–108
Chapter 9	Ships and Boats	109–122
Chapter 10	Magnet Fun	123–132
Chapter 11	How Sound Travels	133–146
Chapter 12	Guide to the Constellations	147–160
Chapter 13	Flying Machines	161–170

To the Teacher

Scott Foresman provides three Leveled Readers for every chapter of *Scott Foresman Science*, Grades 1–6: a *Below-Level Leveled Reader*, an *On-Level Leveled Reader*, and an *Advanced Leveled Reader*.

All three readers teach the same science concepts, same vocabulary, address the same target reading skill and contain the same graphic organizer as the corresponding student edition chapter, just at three different reading levels—providing access to important science content for all students. The On-level and Advanced readers also use additional examples to enrich the chapter and extend ideas

This book contains reproducible copies of the Advanced Leveled Readers for Grade 2. These are designed for you to reproduce and send home with your students as appropriate. Encourage students to share these books with parents or family members in order to practice reading skills and reinforce science content.

Online versions of these and other readers are also available through the Scott Foresman Leveled Reader Database.

Desert Plants

by Michael MacGillivray

Genre	Comprehension Skill	Text Features	Science Content
Nonfiction	Predict	• Captions • Labels • Glossary	Plants

Scott Foresman Science 2.1

ISBN 0-328-13771-5

9 780328 137718

90000

PEARSON

Scott Foresman

scottforesman.com

What did you learn?

Vocabulary	Extended Vocabulary
adapt	cactus
environment	evaporation
flower	oasis
leaf	petals
nutrients	pollination
prairie	surface
roots	
stem	

1. What are the two ways desert plant roots grow?

2. What do spines do?

3. **Writing** in Science Some desert plants have folds in their skin. Write to explain how folds help desert plants store water. Use words from the book as you write.

4. **Predict** What will happen to desert plants after it rains?

Picture Credits

Every effort has been made to secure permission and provide appropriate credit for photographic material.
The publisher deeply regrets any omission and pledges to correct errors called to its attention in subsequent editions.

Photo locators denoted as follows: Top (T), Center (C), Bottom (B), Left (L), Right (R), Background (Bkgd).

Opener: Okapia/OSF/Photolibrary. 2 (R) Digital Vision; 4 David Whitten/Index Stock Imagery; 10 George D. Lepp/Corbis; 15 (TL) Gerry Ellis/Minden Pictures; 17 Okapia/OSF/Photolibrary; 20 Phil Banko/Corbis; 23 Dave G. Houser/Corbis.

Unless otherwise acknowledged, all photographs are the copyright © of Dorling Kindersley, a division of Pearson.

ISBN: 0-328-13771-5

Glossary

cactus	a desert plant with very sharp spines
evaporation	to turn into a gas
oasis	a place in the desert with water and plants
petals	parts of a flower
pollination	carrying pollen from one flower to another so new plants can grow
surface	the top part of something

Desert Plants

by Michael MacGillivray

What You Already Know

The roots of a plant grow into the soil. They hold the plant in place. Roots also take in water and nutrients. Plants need nutrients to live and grow.

The stem holds up the plant. It also brings water and nutrients to the leaves. Leaves use sunlight, water, and air to make food.

young tree

Some plants have flowers. Flowers make fruit and seeds that can grow into new plants. Scattering helps carry seeds to new places where they can grow. Some plants have cones instead of flowers. Their seeds come from the cones.

Desert Plants

Many plants have adapted to grow in hot and dry deserts. Colorful flowers bloom after rain and make the desert come alive. Flowers help make new plants. Desert animals move pollen from flower to flower. This is called pollination. Plants can grow seeds when pollen moves.

Some plants have roots that are near the top of the ground. These plants need to take in rain. Other plants have deep roots that get water from under the ground. Desert plants find many ways to store water. Some plants use spines to keep the water in.

Some desert plants can grow very big and very old. The Joshua tree and the Welwitschia are two of the oldest growing plants. Palm trees grow very tall. They can grow near an oasis. People can live on an oasis if there is enough room.

Deserts may seem empty at first. But if you know where to look, you will find that they are full of life.

The environment of a plant is the place where it lives. Plants have adapted to live in different kinds of places. Prairies, woodlands, and marshes are places where plants can grow.

Deserts are hot and dry environments. Even so, plenty of plants can be found in the desert. Read on to find out how desert plants have adapted to live where it is hot and dry.

Monument Valley, Arizona, USA

Plants in the Desert

There are deserts all over the world. Most deserts are very hot and dry. We think of deserts as empty places full of sand, but most deserts are only partly made of sand. As long as there is water, deserts can be a home for many living things.

Lots of plants can grow in an oasis because there is water. Sometimes, palm trees will grow in an oasis. They stand tall over the land and can be seen from far away. They let people know where an oasis is. If an oasis is large enough, people can live on it.

Another kind of oasis is a stream that starts in the mountains and flows through the desert. Plants also grow along this kind of oasis.

An Oasis

An oasis is a place in the desert with water. The water in an oasis comes from rain or snow high up in the mountains or hills. It travels through rocks under the ground. If the water stops at a low place in the desert, then an oasis can form.

water in an oasis

Most deserts get less than ten inches of rain each year. Some deserts might not get any rain at all for many years. Others get many inches of rain all at once. Even though there is only a little water in these areas, many types of plants live in the desert. These plants depend on rain and underground water to survive.

plants growing in a desert

Quick to Flower

Some parts of a desert can become very colorful after it rains. Many plants make flowers only when it rains. The flowers that bloom hold seeds. New plants can grow from the seeds.

Flower petals lose their water fast in the hot desert sun. The water becomes a gas and goes into the air. This is called evaporation. Petals dry up and fall off when water evaporates from them.

Some plants spring to life when it rains. These plants bloom very quickly. They only live for a few weeks or months after they bloom. The seeds of some of these plants can last up to three years waiting for rain.

flowering cactus

The Joshua tree is an amazing desert plant. The Joshua tree grows to forty feet. One of the oldest Joshua trees is more than nine hundred years old!

The Welwitschia (wehl-WHICH-ee-uh) plant lives even longer than the Joshua tree. It starts with a pair of wide, long leaves. These leaves grow and split. Then it looks like there are more than two leaves. These plants can live to be one to two thousand years old!

Welwitschia plant

Amazing Plants

Joshua tree

It is not easy to live in the desert. Many desert plants are small and have short lives. But some desert plants are amazing because of their big size and long life.

Pollination and Seeds

Some plants use their flowers to make new plants. Their flowers make a fine powder called pollen. Desert animals fly from flower to flower. They carry the pollen from one plant to another. This is called pollination.

Pollen helps new seeds start to grow. Sometimes the seeds are in a fruit that the plant makes. The agave (ah-GAH-vay) cactus has a yellow flower that makes a smooth green fruit. This fruit can hold many seeds.

the yellow flower of an agave cactus

The desert holly is made to live in the dry desert. This plant keeps salt on its prickly leaves. The salt is like a sunblock. It helps the plant stay cooler. The desert holly can sometimes drop its leaves to save water.

The baby-toes cactus has very special leaves. Most of the plant is under the ground, but the leaves stick up. The leaf tips are see-through. They let light into the rest of the leaf.

The glossy green leaves of the desert rose will fall off if the plant does not get enough water. When water can be found, its leaves grow again.

The leaves of the desert rose also help the plant stay safe. The parts of this plant, including the leaves, are poisonous.

desert rose

baby-toes cactus

The century plant can grow to be ten to fourteen feet tall. It has flowers that bloom near the top. The century plant was named by people who thought that it bloomed once every one hundred years. This is not really true. Small century plants can bloom after three or four years. Some big ones bloom after forty or fifty years.

Century plant flowers are mostly yellow.

Roots

Desert plants use their roots to get as much water as they can. Since there is not a lot of water, desert plants grow far apart. This way, the roots do not have to fight each other for the little bit of water that there is.

Some plants have roots that grow near the surface or top of the ground. These roots spread out. They take in water when it rains. Other plants have roots that grow deep into the earth. These plants take in underground water. A plant with deep roots can get water more of the time. It does not have to wait for rain.

All plants must share water.

The kookerboom tree only grows leaves at the top of its branches.

Most cactus plants do not have leaves. Plants without leaves use their stems to make food.

Cactus plants have sharp spines. The spines grow on the plant's skin. Spines block the wind. They can also keep the Sun off the plant with their tiny shadows. In these ways they help keep water in the plant.

kookerboom leaves

Leaves and Spines

Plants lose water in the Sun and wind. The leaves of desert plants are made to keep water in. Many desert plants only have a few leaves. Others have small leaves. Some plants drop their leaves when it gets too dry. Other plants have leaves with small holes to take in water. The holes open at night, when it is cooler, and close during the day, when it is hotter.

Some desert plants have leaves. Some do not.

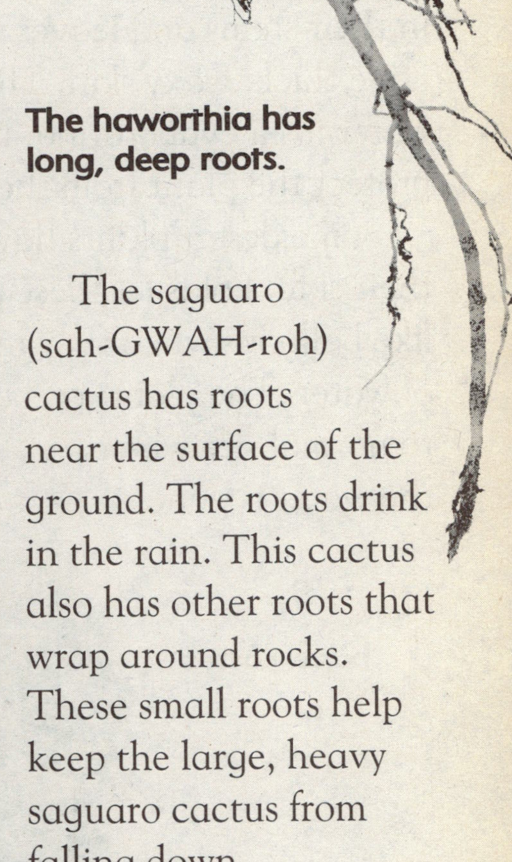

The haworthia has long, deep roots.

The saguaro (sah-GWAH-roh) cactus has roots near the surface of the ground. The roots drink in the rain. This cactus also has other roots that wrap around rocks. These small roots help keep the large, heavy saguaro cactus from falling down.

Storing Water

Cactus plants grow in many deserts. A cactus is a plant that has special ways to store water. Many plants store water in their stems and leaves. Cactus plants have thick, waxy skin. This skin keeps water from evaporating. It also helps protect the plant from the Sun.

Some desert plants have folds in their skin. Folds let these plants grow like balloons when they take in a lot of water. The plants go back to normal size when the water is gone.

barrel cactus

The skin of a barrel cactus has folds and tough spines. The spines grow in bunches. The barrel cactus can store a lot of water. It gets bigger when it holds water. It grows slowly and can live more than one hundred years.

Nocturnal Animals

by Ann M. Rossi

15

Genre	Comprehension Skill	Text Features	Science Content
Nonfiction	Alike and Different	• Labels • Call Outs • Glossary	Vertebrates and Invertebrates

Scott Foresman Science 2.2

Vocabulary

amphibian
bird
camouflage
fish
gills
insect
mammal
reptile

Extended Vocabulary

arachnids
burrows
carnivores
echolocation
nocturnal
talons

What did you learn?

1. How is a desert hamster adapted to live in its environment?

2. What does a scorpion eat?

3. **Writing** in Science Red-eyed tree frogs have ways to stay safe. Write to explain how they avoid predators. Use details from the book to support your answer.

4. **Alike and Different** How is an owl like a firefly? How is it different?

Picture Credits
Every effort has been made to secure permission and provide appropriate credit for photographic material. The publisher deeply regrets any omission and pledges to correct errors called to its attention in subsequent editions.

Photo locators denoted as follows: Top (T), Center (C), Bottom (B), Left (L), Right (R), Background (Bkgd).

3: © Natural History Museum, London/DK Images; 4-5: © Stocktrek/Corbis; 9: © Michael and Patricia Fogden/Corbis; 10: © Maslowski Photo/DK Images; 11: © Kim Taylor/ DK Images; 12: © Darwin Dale/Photoresearchers, Inc.; 13: © Brian Brake/Photoresearchers, Inc.; 14: Bob Bennett/Photolibrary.com; 15: © RO-MA Stock/Index Stock Imagery; 18: © Jerry Young/DK Images; 21: © Natural History Museum/DK Images; 21 (BR): © Jerry Young/DK Images. Cover: © Darwin Dale/Photoresearchers, Inc.

Unless otherwise acknowledged, all photographs are the copyright © of Dorling Kindersley, a division of Pearson.

ISBN: 0-328-13774-X

Glossary

arachnids	animals with four pairs of legs and two main body parts
burrows	holes or tunnels dug by small animals and used as homes or shelters
carnivores	meat-eating animals
echolocation	the way animals such as bats and dolphins use their senses to find other objects in their environment
nocturnal	most active at night
talons	the claws of predatory birds like owls and eagles

Nocturnal Animals

by Ann M. Rossi

What You Already Know

There are many different kinds of animals. The different kinds of animals can be put into groups.

One group of animals has backbones. Mammals have backbones. So do most birds, fish, reptiles, and amphibians.

Another group of animals does not have backbones. Insects do not have backbones.

Animals in all groups are adapted to different kinds of environments.

beetle

Each kind of animal has special adaptations that help it live in its environment. But nocturnal creatures are alike in one very important way. They are all adapted for life at night.

Nocturnal animals are found in many different environments. Nocturnal animals live on the ground, in the air, and in the ocean. Some of these creatures are adapted for life where it is hot. Others are adapted for life where it is cold. Nocturnal animals can live where it is wet and where it is dry.

Some animals change color to hide from predators. This is one kind of camouflage. Fish are adapted to live in water. Fish have gills to help them get oxygen from the water. Each animal is adapted to live in its environment.

The animals in this book are also adapted to live in their environment. They are adapted to hunt and be active at night.

moth

Nocturnal Animals

Have you ever been outside at night and heard animal noises? Maybe you have seen an animal moving around in the dark. Maybe you have heard animal noises near you. Not all animals sleep at night. Some animals rest in the daytime and use the night for finding food and hunting prey.

There are also many nocturnal animals that do not have backbones. The moth is a nocturnal insect. The earthworm is a nocturnal worm.

moth

crocodile

There are nocturnal creatures in almost every group of animals. There are many nocturnal animals that have backbones. The panther is a nocturnal mammal. The kiwi is a nocturnal bird. The angel shark is a nocturnal fish. The crocodile is a nocturnal reptile. The toad is a nocturnal amphibian.

panther

Animals that find food and move around at night are called nocturnal animals. Nocturnal animals can be found in many different habitats. Animals such as desert hamsters, scorpions, owls, fireflies, coyotes, bats, and red-eyed tree frogs are nocturnal.

Desert Hamsters

Desert hamsters are small mammals that live in the desert. They are well adapted to life in this environment. Desert hamsters want to keep out of the heat and light of the desert in the daytime. They dig underground burrows. Each desert hamster spends the daytime hours sleeping in its own deep burrow.

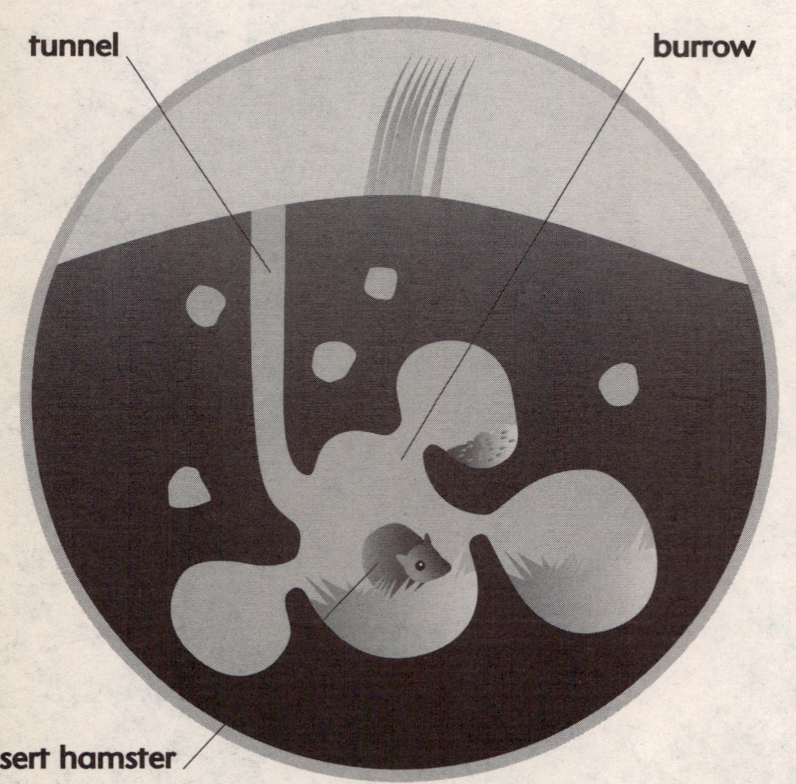

Red-eyed tree frogs live in trees. When they sleep during the day, their green coloring helps to camouflage them in the leaves. This way, they can try to stay safe from predators that hunt in the daytime.

Sometimes, predators are not fooled by the red-eyed tree frog's camouflage. If a predator gets too close, the frog wakes up. When the frog's eyes pop open, their shining red color scares away the predator.

Desert hamsters come out of their burrows at night to find food. Their back feet are furry to protect them from hot desert sand. Desert hamsters eat seeds. They also eat fruit, leaves, stems, and buds. Sometimes, desert hamsters eat insects.

Red-eyed Tree Frogs

The red-eyed tree frog is another nocturnal animal. Like some bats, the red-eyed tree frog lives in a tropical environment. This kind of amphibian lives in rain forests in Central and South America.

Red-eyed tree frogs hunt for prey at night. Like some of the other animals you have read about, red-eyed tree frogs are carnivores. They eat crickets, moths, flies, grasshoppers, and even other frogs.

Scorpions

Scorpions also live in the desert. Scorpions might look like insects, but they are arachnids. Arachnids have four sets of legs and two body parts. Spiders, mites, and ticks are also arachnids.

Like desert hamsters, scorpions spend the daytime out of the hot desert sun. During the day, scorpions find cool, shady places to sleep. They sleep in cracks of wood. They sleep inside and under rocks.

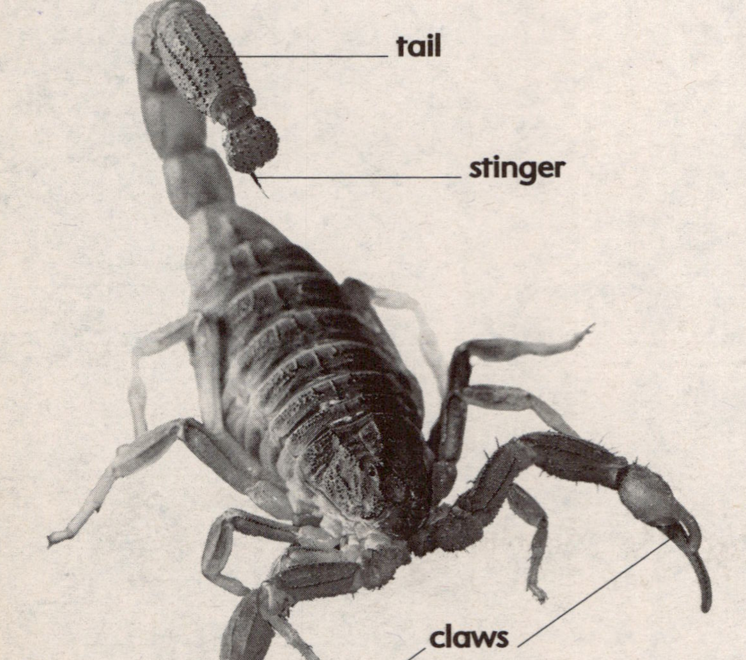

Bats eat all kinds of food. Some bats eat insects, scorpions, or spiders. Others eat fruit. There are even bats that catch fish, lizards, small birds, or tree frogs. Bats can find food on the ground, on plants, and in the air.

Many bats use their sense of smell to find food. Others use echolocation. This means that when these bats fly they make sounds that echo, or bounce off, objects. The bat can tell where the objects are. This way, they can find their prey in the dark.

Bats

What is that animal hanging upside-down? It is a bat! These flying mammals are also nocturnal. They live in many different habitats too.

Most bats hang upside-down to rest in the daytime. They may sleep in trees, caves, or attics. Some kinds of bats sleep hanging by one foot!

At night, scorpions come out to look for food. They eat insects, spiders, centipedes, earthworms, and other scorpions. They use their claws to catch their prey. Scorpions inject poison into their prey with the stinger in their tail.

Owls

Not all nocturnal animals live in the desert. Owls live in many different habitats. During the day, they sleep in hollow trees or holes in rocky cliffs.

When night comes, owls are ready to go hunting. They see and hear well in the dark. Some owls can find mice just by hearing them run.

Coyotes spend most nights hunting in groups of twos and threes. Coyotes will eat almost anything they are able to chew. They eat rabbits, squirrels, other small mammals, insects, reptiles, and fruit.

Coyotes hear well. They listen to find prey and to keep away from danger.

These birds are carnivores, or meat eaters.
Most owls catch live animals to eat, like mice,
gophers, and small birds. They swoop down
silently. They use their claws, called talons,
to grab their prey. Some kinds of owls look for
prey while flying high in the air. Other kinds
stay low to the ground when they hunt.

Coyotes

Do you know what these animals are?
They are coyotes! Like owls and fireflies, coyotes
live in many different habitats. These nocturnal
mammals spend most days sleeping in dens.
Coyotes usually dig their own dens. Sometimes,
they will take holes made by other animals and
make them bigger. Sometimes, coyotes will make
dens in holes in rocky ledges.

Fireflies

Fireflies also fly around at night looking for food. These nocturnal insects live in many habitats, but most fireflies are found in warm damp places.

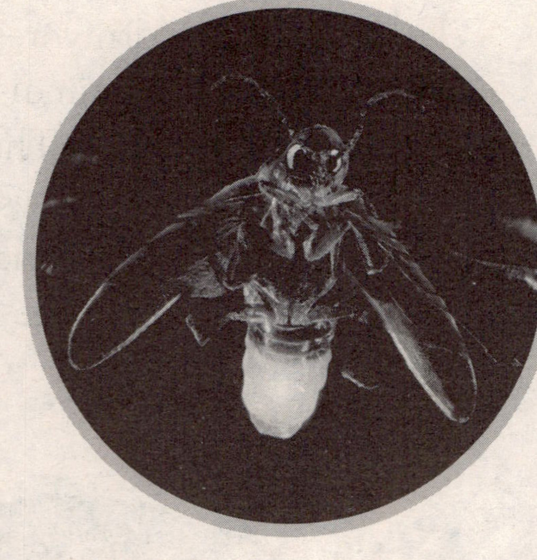

Fireflies mostly live near streams and ponds. They spend their days sleeping in bushes near the water. The fireflies on the right live in a cave.

At night, young fireflies look for earthworms, snails, and slugs to eat. Older fireflies eat plant nectar.

Have you ever seen a firefly at night? Flickering lights can be seen as they zip through the night sky. They have body parts that can give off a light signal. This light helps them warn away predators. It also helps them communicate with other fireflies.

LIFE IN A RAIN FOREST

by Shirley Horton

Genre	Comprehension Skill	Text Features	Science Content
Nonfiction	Cause and Effect	• Captions • Map • Labels • Glossary	Plants and Animals

Scott Foresman Science 2.3

What did you learn?

Vocabulary	Extended Vocabulary
consumer	algae
food chain	emergent
food web	equator
predator	layers
prey	nectar
producer	pollen

1. What are the layers of a rain forest?

2. How do archer fish get food?

3. **Writing** in Science   Monkeys live in the canopy of the rain forest. Write to explain how their bodies help them live in the trees. Use words from this book as you write.

4. **Cause and Effect** What might happen if a bird or a lizard gets too close to a boa?

Picture Credits
Every effort has been made to secure permission and provide appropriate credit for photographic material.
The publisher deeply regrets any omission and pledges to correct errors called to its attention in subsequent editions.

Photo locators denoted as follows: Top (T), Center (C), Bottom (B), Left (L), Right (R), Background (Bkgd).

9 (B) Stephen Dalton/NHPA Limited; 12 (C) Neil Nightingale/Nature Picture Library,
(R) Terry Whittaker/Frank Lane Picture Agency/Corbis; 13 (B) ©Jerry Young/DK Images.

Scott Foresman/Dorling Kindersley would also like to thank: 16 (B) Jerry Young/DK Images;
18 (R) Jerry Young/DK Images.

Unless otherwise acknowledged, all photographs are the copyright © of Dorling Kindersley, a division of Pearson.

ISBN: 0-328-13777-4

Glossary

algae   tiny plants that grow in water

emergent   coming up into the sunlight

equator   an imaginary circle around the middle of the Earth

layers   parts that go on top of one another

nectar   a sweet liquid found in many flowers

pollen   a fine powder that comes from flowers

LIFE IN A RAIN FOREST

by Shirley Horton

31

What You Already Know

Plants and animals need each other to live. Sometimes plants and animals help each other find food and shelter. Sometimes they protect each other. Sometimes they eat each other!

Plants make food with energy from the Sun. Many animals eat plants. Other animals eat these animals. This is called a food chain.

Living things that make their own food, like plants, are called producers. Animals that eat other living things are called consumers. Some animals hunt other animals for food. They are called predators. Some animals get hunted. They are called prey. Food chains have predators and prey.

rainbow lorikeet

If you ever visit a rain forest, watch for these beautiful birds and for the other animals you have read about. You will not see them all in the same rain forest. At first, you may not even see any of them. But keep watching. Some of them will be watching you!

These birds are parrots. They fly through the emergent layer to find food. They make loud noises as they fly. Parrots and their eggs are the prey of many forest animals. They are also hunted by people who sell them as pets.

parakeet

macaw

A food web is when many food chains happen in one place. Food webs are found in many environments. Sometimes food webs change.

In this book you will read about how plants and animals live together in a rain forest. You will learn about the parts of a rain forest. You will meet many different plants and animals that live in each part.

This chameleon is using its long tongue to catch an insect.

What is a rain forest?

Look at the map below. The red line is the equator. It is an imaginary line that goes all around the middle of the world. Right over and under the line is where rain forests grow.

Plants in these forests grow tall, thick, and green. This is because the weather there is warm and wet.

There are different layers in a rain forest, like the layers of a cake.

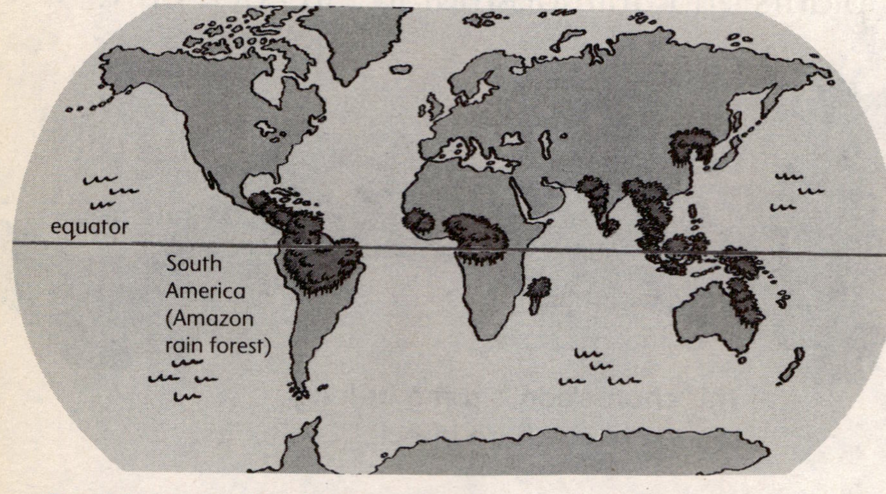

On this map, the dark green places are rain forests.

Marmosets are little monkeys that eat insects and fruit. They can move through the treetops. They cannot hold on with their tails and hands as well as other monkeys.

Colobus monkeys almost never go down to the floor of the forest. They find most of the food they eat in the trees. These monkeys have very long tails to help them move in the trees.

colobus monkey

The Emergent Layer

Rain forest butterflies fly in the emergent layer. The blue morpho butterfly is easy to spot. It is bright blue. Predators are fooled by the way this butterfly looks. Predators think it is a flower. They stay away and the butterfly stays safe.

blue morpho butterfly

marmoset

Rain Forest Layers

The River

Many kinds of fish live and lay their eggs in the rivers of rain forests. Most fish eat insects that fall into the water. Archer fish do not wait for their dinner to come to them. They knock insects off low-hanging plants. Then, gulp!

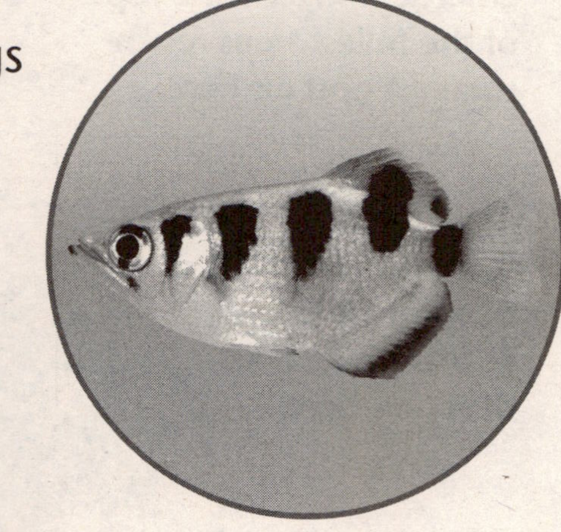

archer fish

caiman crocodile

Monkeys can stay safe in their treetop homes. As long as they stay up in the trees, they cannot be eaten!

Gibbons are small apes. They are like monkeys in many ways but they have no tails.

siamang gibbon

Monkeys live in the canopy too. These animals swing and leap through their treetop homes. They are made to move well in the trees. They have long arms and tails. They have hands and feet that can grip the branches.

squirrel monkey

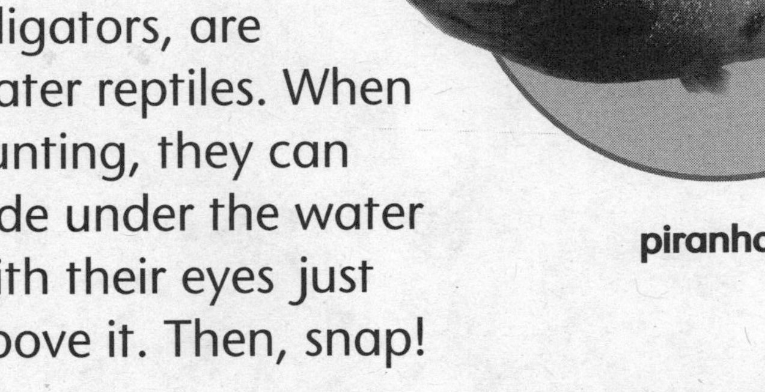

spider monkey

Piranhas are fast fish with lots of very sharp teeth. They like nibbling the fins of other fish for food. Snip, snip!

Caimans, like alligators, are water reptiles. When hunting, they can hide under the water with their eyes just above it. Then, snap!

piranha

The Riverbank

Tapirs are mammals. They look
for plants to eat at night. They
have to be careful when they look
for food. Predators, such as large
snakes and water reptiles,
are watching for
tapirs to eat!

tapir

Many swinging
and flying animals
live in the canopy.
Tiny green plants
called algae
grow in the hair
of big sloths.
These plants grow
because a sloth's fur
is wet from the rain.

Unlike other canopy
birds, toucans have very long
beaks. Their beaks are long,
but they are very light.

toucan

38

The Canopy

Lots of different kinds of orchids grow in the canopy. People around the world love these beautiful flowers. People take these flowers to many other places to grow.

orchid

sloth

Anacondas are big snakes. Sometimes they hunt for food in the river. Other times they hunt in the trees. Anacondas coil around their prey. Then they swallow their prey in one big gulp.

Basilisk lizards are small, light, and fast. These reptiles can run across the water on their back legs as they chase their food.

anaconda

basilisk lizard

The Forest

Gorillas are big apes that live in lowland or mountain rain forests. They spend their days playing, sleeping, and eating on the forest floor. At night, young gorillas sleep in nests in the trees. Other gorillas build their nests on the ground.

gorilla

golden tree boa

Chameleons are lizards. They change their colors to look like the forest around them. This camouflage helps them stay safe.

Boas are snakes that curl up in tree branches. They trap birds and lizards that get too close. Then they strike, squeeze, and swallow.

Many plants growing from branches in the understory are shaped like cups. These plants can hold rainwater. Tree frogs lay their eggs in these plant cups. The frogs also hide in these plants to wait for insects to fly by. They eat the insects they catch.

red-eyed tree frog

chameleon

Insects and spiders also live on the forest floor. Wasps and bees drink nectar from forest flowers. They carry pollen from flower to flower. This helps fruit to grow.

Tarantulas are big spiders. They move fast through the leaves on the forest floor. They have hair all over!

paper wasps

tarantula

Some flowers grow on the dark forest floor. Rafflesia (rah-FLEE-zhah) flowers have no stems or leaves. They live on the roots or stems of other plants. Rafflesias are the largest flowers ever found.

rafflesia

The Understory

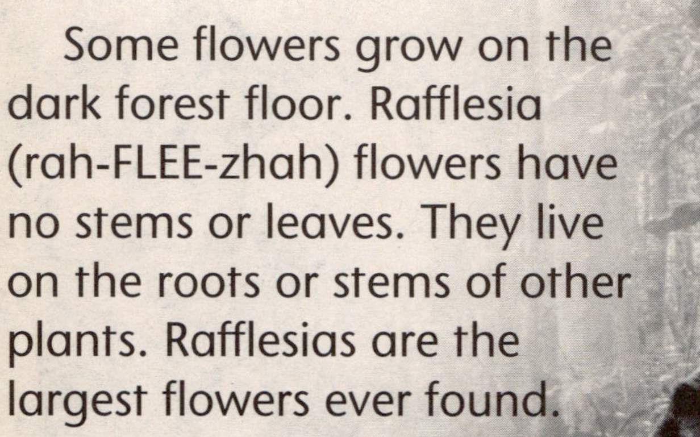

Some of the animals that live among the leaves, branches, and vines of the understory never go down to the forest floor. Bats sleep in the day, hanging from branches. At night they zip through the trees hunting for food. Some bats eat only insects. Others, like this vampire bat, eat animal blood.

vampire bat

Animal Eggs

by Molly Fleck

Genre	Comprehension Skill	Text Features	Science Content
Nonfiction	Infer	• Call Outs • Captions • Labels • Glossary	Living Things

Scott Foresman Science 2.4

Vocabulary	Extended Vocabulary
germinate	egg tooth
life cycle	hatch
nymph	incubate
seed coat	larva
seedling	metamorphosis
	oviparous

What did you learn?

1. What two sources of food does a bird egg provide for a young bird?

2. Where do most frogs lay their eggs?

3. **Writing** in Science Some young animals have an egg tooth. Write to explain what an egg tooth does. Use examples from this book to support your answer.

4. **Infer** What are crabs most likely to do with their eggs until they hatch?

Picture Credits
Every effort has been made to secure permission and provide appropriate credit for photographic material.
The publisher deeply regrets any omission and pledges to correct errors called to its attention in subsequent editions.

Photo locators denoted as follows: Top (T), Center (C), Bottom (B), Left (L), Right (R), Background (Bkgd).

15 (T) M. Watson/Ardea.

Unless otherwise acknowledged, all photographs are the copyright © of Dorling Kindersley, a division of Pearson.

ISBN: 0-328-13780-4

Animal Eggs

by Molly Fleck

Glossary

egg tooth   a special tooth that helps some young animals break out of their egg

hatch   when a young animal breaks out of its egg

incubate   keep warm to help hatch

larvae   young animals that change through metamorphosis to become adults

metamorphosis changing from a nymph or a larva into an adult

oviparous   egg-laying

What You Already Know

Living things grow in different ways. Different kinds of plants and animals have different life cycles.

Most plants grow from seeds. A seed coat protects the seed. It also protects the tiny plant and the stored food that are inside the seed. A seed will germinate when it gets enough water and air. The seed will first grow into a seedling. That seedling will then grow into an adult plant.

Some animals lay eggs. Others do not. Animals such as the sea turtle and dragonfly lay eggs. Young mammals grow inside their mothers.

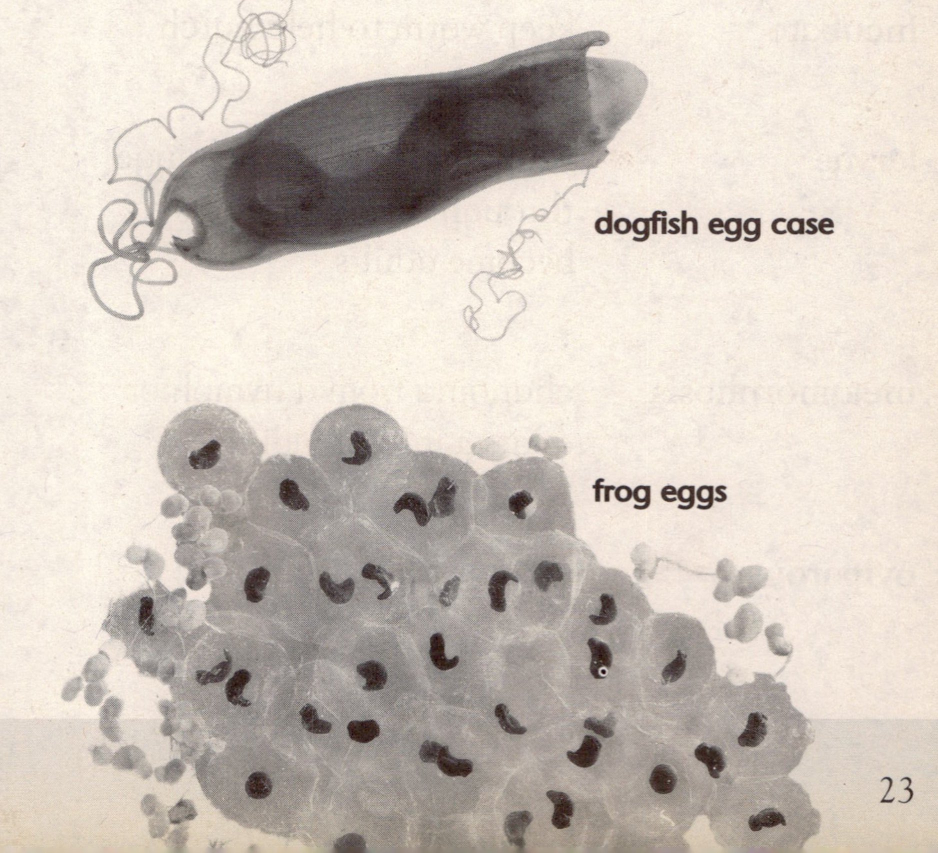

Bean plants grow from seeds.

Some animals guard their eggs to keep them safe. Many young animals hatch on their own.

Eggs contain the food a young animal needs to live. For many animals, an egg is the perfect place to grow.

ladybug eggs

dogfish egg case

frog eggs

Many Different Eggs

Eggs come in many different sizes, colors, and shapes. Animals lay eggs in many different places. They lay eggs in water, in nests, below the ground, or on the ground. Some eggs are held in a glob of jelly. Others have a hard covering, such as a shell.

Some animals stay with their eggs until they hatch. Birds incubate their eggs so the young will grow.

snake hatching

duck hatching

Sea turtles live in the ocean. They crawl onto beaches to dig their nests and lay their eggs. Young sea turtles look just like their parents.

Dragonflies often lay their eggs in the water. Nymphs hatch from dragonfly eggs. They look different from their parents, and they have no wings. As nymphs grow, they shed their skin. They will grow wings by the time they reach adulthood.

This book is about many different kinds of animal eggs. You will learn about the kinds of animals that lay eggs, how some animals keep their eggs safe, and how eggs hatch.

This dragonfly has just shed its skin.

All About Eggs

Eggs keep the young animals that are growing inside them safe. They also provide food. When the young animal inside the egg is ready to hatch, it breaks out of the shell.

Birds, fish, reptiles, and amphibians lay eggs. Most insects lay eggs too. Different kinds of animals lay their eggs in different environments. Young animals can grow safely inside the eggs.

bird eggs

corn snake hatching

Cod, herring, and many other fish do not stay with their eggs. However, some kinds of fish keep their eggs safe.

Trout cover their eggs with gravel before they leave them. Sticklebacks guard their eggs until they hatch. Brown bullheads will protect their young after they hatch. Some kinds of fish even carry their eggs in their mouths until they hatch.

dogfish hatching

a bullhead protecting its eggs

Fish Eggs

Some fish eggs are light. They are so light that they float on the top of the water. Other fish eggs are heavy and sink to the bottom of the water. Many fish eggs become food for hungry predators.

Some fish grow into adults in minutes. Others take years to become adults.

goldfish egg

goldfish hatching

A goldfish takes four years to become an adult.

Eggs come in many different shapes, sizes, and colors. Some animals lay just one egg at a time. Other animals lay many eggs at once.

Bird eggs have a hard, protective shell. Many bird eggs are oval shaped. They may be a solid color or have spots on them.

Most frogs lay their eggs in water. Frogs lay a lot of eggs. Their eggs stay held in a glob of jelly. Insects such as moths and butterflies usually lay their eggs in clusters. They will sometimes lay them on leaves.

frog eggs

butterfly eggs

Growth And Development

Eggs need to be kept still and warm. Otherwise, the young animals inside them will not be able to develop and hatch. Birds incubate, or warm, their eggs by sitting on them. Most eggs get incubated in a nest. A hen incubates her eggs for twenty-one days before they hatch. The emperor penguin holds its eggs on top of its feet, under the feathers of its belly.

A hen keeps her eggs warm.

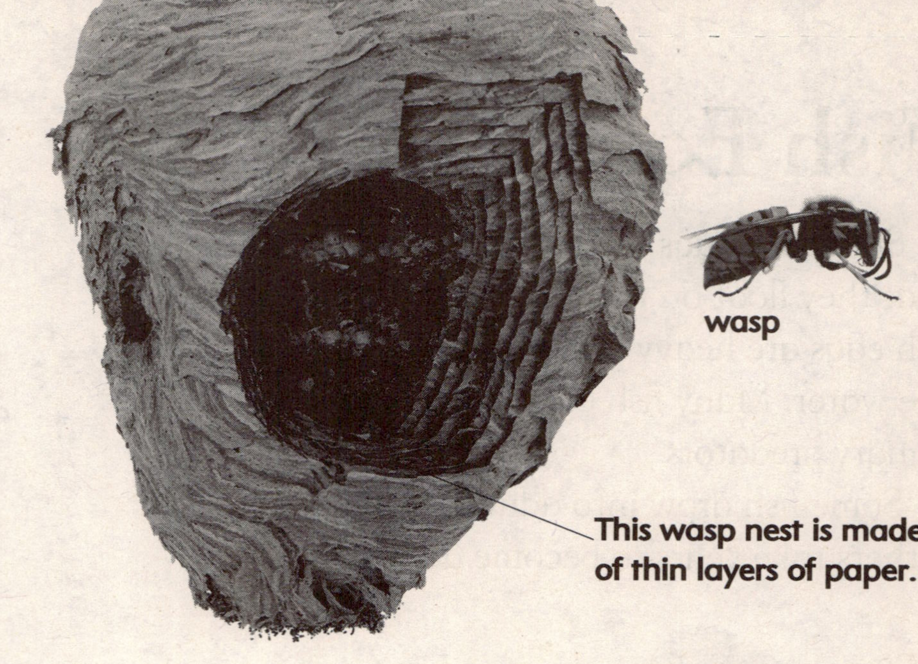
wasp

This wasp nest is made of thin layers of paper.

Insects lay many eggs at a time. Termites can lay up to thirty thousand eggs a day! Insects lay their eggs in many places, often on or near food. When the young hatch, their first meal is nearby.

Some wasps chew plants to make paper. They use the paper to build nests. Then they lay their eggs in the nest.

A ladybug lays its eggs on a leaf.

Insect Eggs

Insect eggs are very small. They come in many different shapes and colors. Most insect eggs are oval or round shaped. The eggs are usually white, or close to white, in color.

Some newly hatched insects look like their parents, only smaller. Others look different from their parents. These young insects are called nymphs or larvae. Their look changes as they grow into adults.

dragonfly

dragonfly eggs

Dragonfly nymphs do not fly. Soon the nymph will become a winged, flying adult.

dragonfly nymph

Many animals do not incubate their eggs. Instead they find a sheltered spot to lay their eggs. Eggs will often be laid beneath a rock or log.

Most turtles lay eggs in nests that they have dug. They throw soil on the nest to hide it. If a predator does not find the nest, the young turtles inside the eggs will develop and hatch.

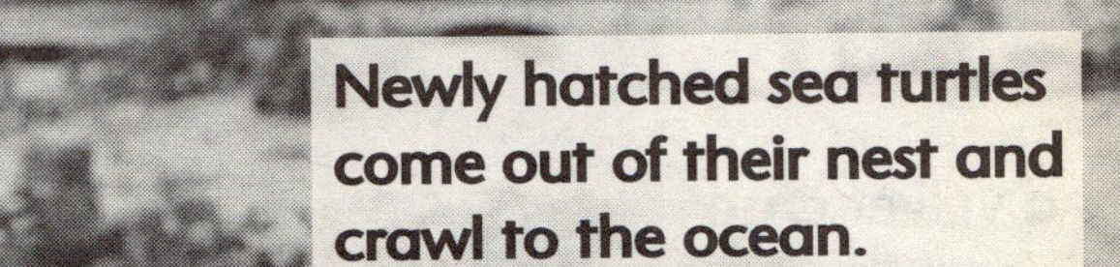

turtle egg

Newly hatched sea turtles come out of their nest and crawl to the ocean.

Protection

Animals have many ways to keep eggs safe from predators or bad weather. Some animals use their bodies to shelter their eggs. Male seahorses carry their eggs in a pouch on the front of their bodies.

Crabs, shrimp, and lobsters are animals with many legs and a hard shell-like covering. They carry their eggs on their bellies and keep them safe until they hatch.

a velvet crab carrying its eggs

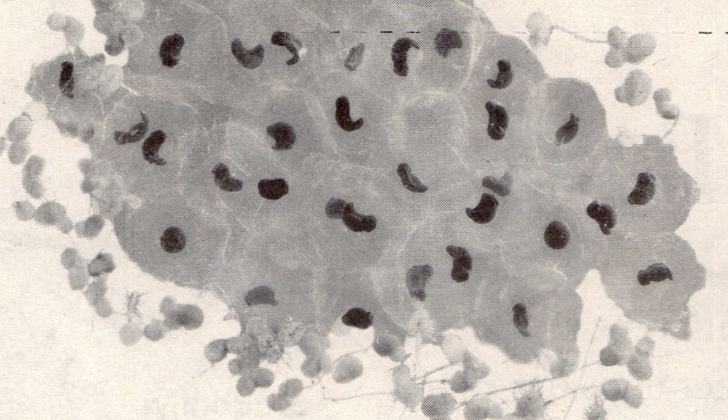
Amphibian eggs are protected by gel-like blobs.

Most amphibians lay a lot of eggs all at once. Large bullfrogs may lay as many as forty-five thousand eggs at the same time!

A lot of amphibians do not stay with their eggs. Some frogs and toads, such as the male midwife toad, lay their eggs on land. They carry their eggs to water to hatch. One kind of Australian frog swallows its eggs. When the eggs hatch, the adult opens its mouth to let the young frogs out.

A male midwife toad carries its eggs until they hatch.

Amphibian Eggs

Most amphibians lay their eggs in water or moist ground. Amphibian eggs are held together in a glob of jelly. Most amphibians hatch as larvae. When larvae turn into adults they change a lot! This big change is called metamorphosis.

Newts hatch as larvae in water. When they change into adults they can live on land.

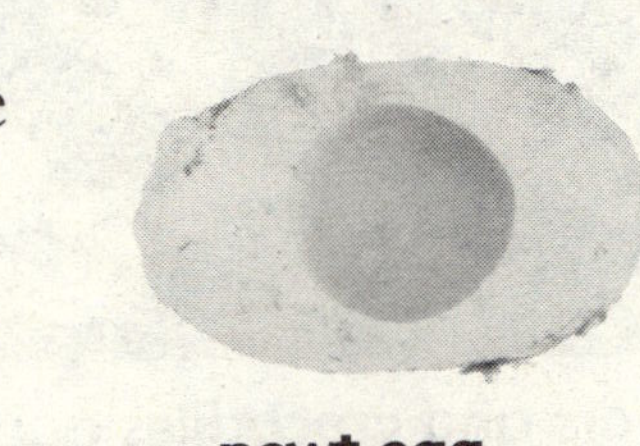
newt egg

newt hatching

an adult newt after it has gone through metamorphosis

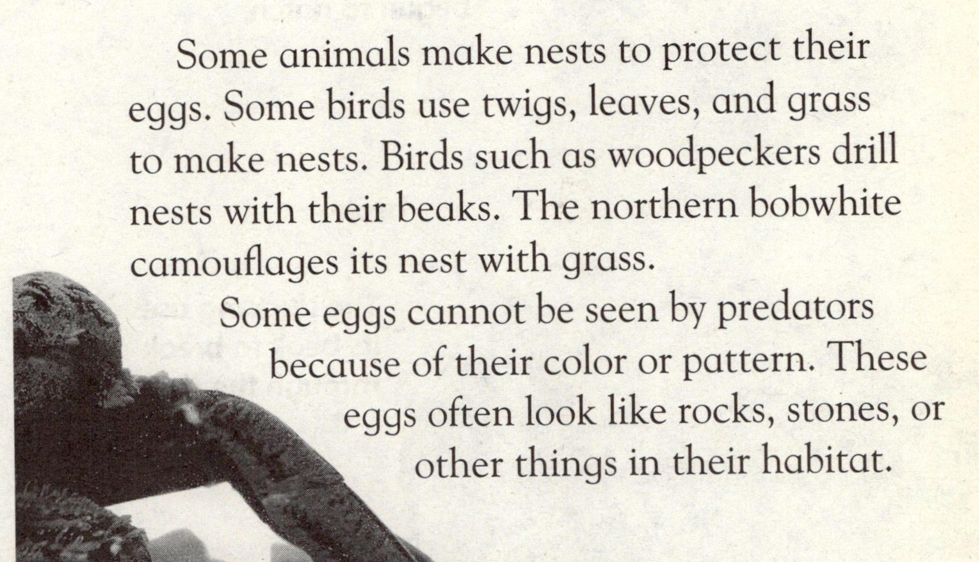
eggs in a
teal duck nest

a camouflaged
quail's egg nest

Some animals make nests to protect their eggs. Some birds use twigs, leaves, and grass to make nests. Birds such as woodpeckers drill nests with their beaks. The northern bobwhite camouflages its nest with grass.

Some eggs cannot be seen by predators because of their color or pattern. These eggs often look like rocks, stones, or other things in their habitat.

Hatching Out

While a mother or father bird is busy keeping its eggs warm, the young bird inside is growing. It feeds off the egg white and egg yolk. For the first two weeks, the young bird eats the egg white. After that, it eats the egg yolk.

A duckling has begun to hatch.

beak

The duckling uses its beak to break through the shell.

Alligators and crocodiles guard their nests.

Alligator and crocodile eggs are hard, like bird eggs. Snake eggs have tough, leathery shells. The eggshells stretch as the young snakes grow.

Young snakes have a special tooth on their upper jaw. Like some birds, they lose their special tooth after they hatch.

corn snake hatching

A newly hatched duckling is wet.

Young birds use their beaks to break out of their shells and hatch. Many chicks have a special tooth called an egg tooth. This hard, sharp bump helps the chick break through the eggshell. The egg tooth falls off after the chick hatches.

This duckling is two days old.

Reptile Eggs

Most reptiles are oviparous. This means they lay eggs. Some reptiles lay only one egg at a time, but others lay hundreds! Many reptiles dig nests or hide their eggs. Some reptiles remain near their eggs. Other reptiles, such as tortoises, leave their eggs to hatch.

After a tortoise has laid her eggs, they usually take about one year to hatch. The young tortoise grows up inside the egg. When the young tortoise is ready, it uses its beak to break the shell. It takes about ten hours for a tortoise to fully hatch.

day 1, 8:30 P.M.

day 2, 4:30 A.M.

A leopard tortoise hatches from its egg.

day 2, 6:20 A.M.

Bird Eggs

Bird eggs come in many shapes and sizes. Ostrich eggs are round. Their shells are thick. Ostriches lay the biggest bird eggs in the world. Each egg weighs about three pounds! Hummingbirds lay the smallest eggs. A hummingbird egg is about the size of a pea.

hummingbird eggs

ostrich egg

starling

hen

cuckoo

oystercatcher

peregrine falcon

Bird eggs come in many shapes, sizes, and colors.

The color and shape of bird eggs may be adapted to their environment. Some birds lay their eggs on the ground. The eggs of these birds have spots. The spots camouflage the eggs.

Some birds, such as the guillemot (GIL-uh-mot), nest on cliffs. Their eggs are pointy at one end. This pointy shape keeps the eggs from rolling off the cliffs.

guillemot eggs

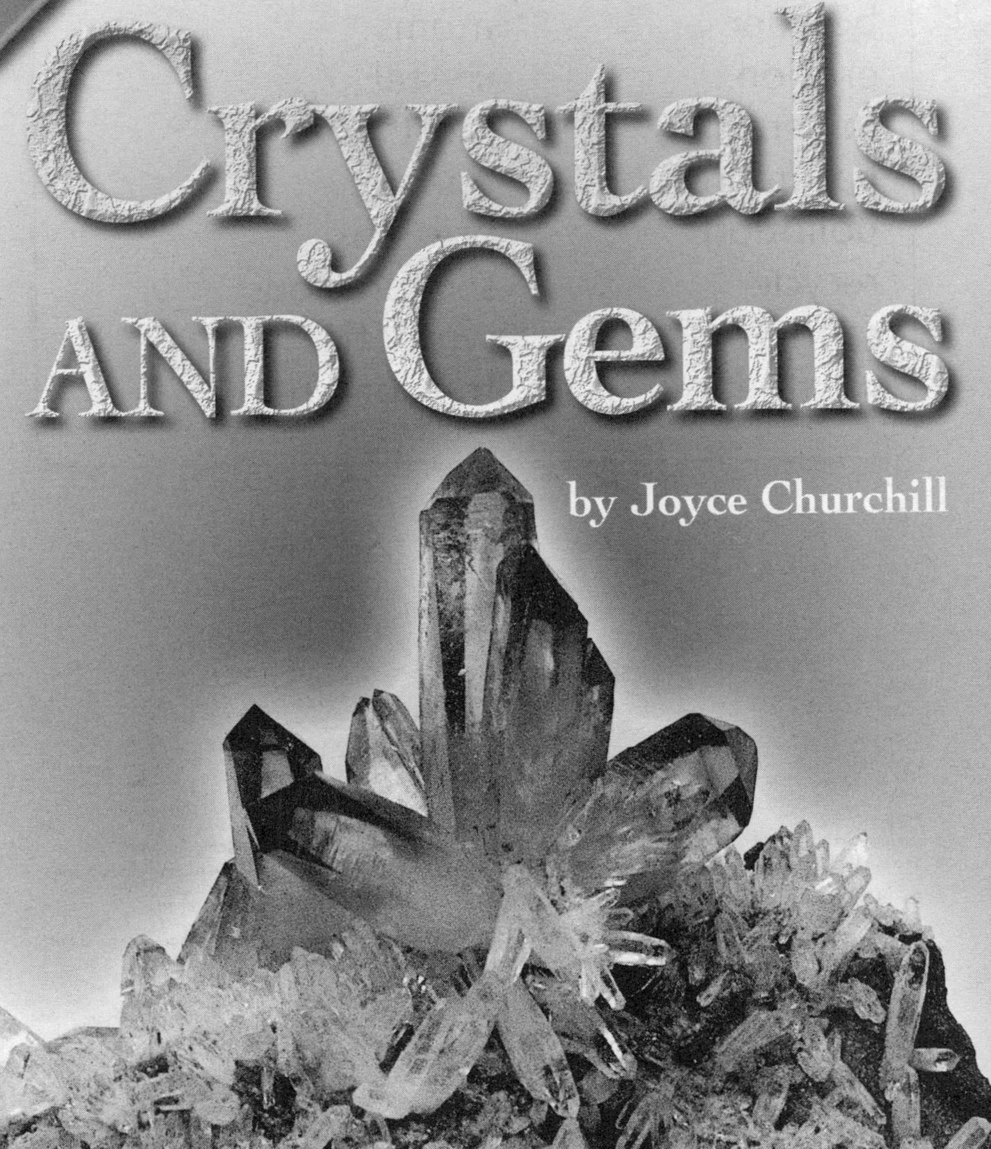

Crystals AND Gems

by Joyce Churchill

Genre	Comprehension Skill	Text Features	Science Content
Nonfiction	Picture Clues	• Captions • Labels • Glossary	Natural Resources

Scott Foresman Science 2.5

PEARSON
Scott Foresman

DK

ISBN 0-328-13783-9

90000

9 780328 137831

scottforesman.com

Vocabulary	Extended Vocabulary
boulder	atoms
erosion	crystal
minerals	facets
natural resource	opaque
pollution	precious
recycle	semiprecious
sand	synthetic
weathering	transparent

What did you learn?

1. What is the difference between transparent and opaque gems?

2. Name two gemstones that come from ancient plants.

3. **Writing** in Science In this book you read about diamonds. Write to explain how diamonds are found and turned into gemstones. Use words from the book as you write.

4. **Picture Clues** Which mineral is harder, gypsum or quartz? Use the Mohs Hardness Scale on pages 8 and 9 to answer this question.

Picture Credits
Every effort has been made to secure permission and provide appropriate credit for photographic material. The publisher deeply regrets any omission and pledges to correct errors called to its attention in subsequent editions.

Photo locators denoted as follows: Top (T), Center (C), Bottom (B), Left (L), Right (R), Background (Bkgd).

Scott Foresman/Dorling Kindersley would like to thank the Natural History Museum, London/DK Images for the use of photos on pages Opener, 4 (BC), 5 (C), 7 (TR, BC, BR), 8 (BL, BCL, BCR, BR), 9 (BL, BCL, BC, CRB, CR), 10 (TL), 12 (CR), 13 (CR), 14 (BR), 16 (BL), 17 (TL), 21 (TCL, TC, TR, CRA, CRB, BCR, BC, BCL, CLB, CL, CLA, TCL), 22 (TR), 23 (CR, B).

Unless otherwise acknowledged, all photographs are the copyright © of Dorling Kindersley, a division of Pearson.

ISBN: 0-328-13783-9

Copyright © Pearson Education, Inc.

Crystals and Gems

by Joyce A. Churchill

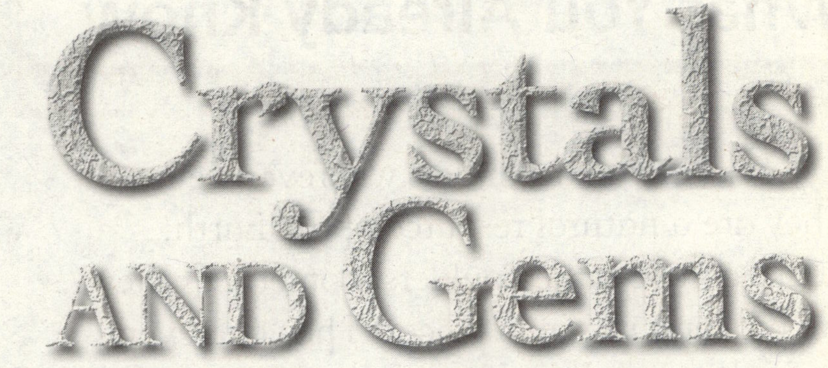

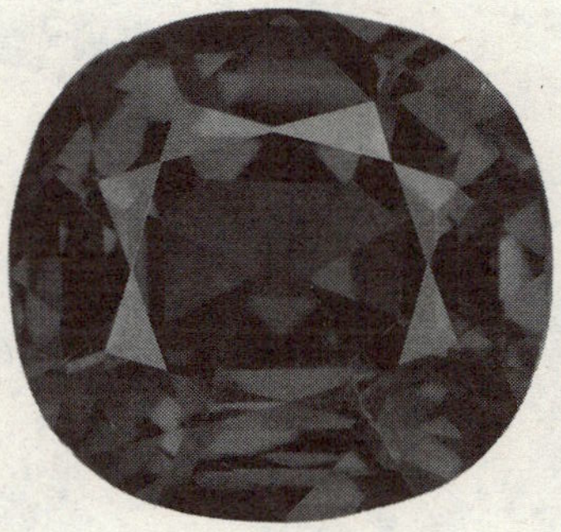

Glossary

atoms	the smallest parts of all things
crystal	a group of atoms in a pattern
facets	sides cut into a gemstone
opaque	something you cannot see through, like milk
precious	the most rare and valuable gemstones
semiprecious	the less rare and less valuable gemstones
synthetic	something made by people and machines
transparent	clear, see-through

What You Already Know

Rocks are all around us wherever we live. They are a natural resource of the Earth. Rocks can be large boulders. Sometimes they are broken into small pieces. They can even be finely ground up, like sand.

Proustite is a crystal mineral that is purple like amethyst.

Gemstones that are rare are called precious stones. Those that are more easily found are called semiprecious stones.

People have valued gemstones for thousands of years. They are some of our most beautiful natural resources.

amethyst

Our Hidden Treasure

Rocks are made up of minerals. Minerals are found all over the Earth.

Gemstones are a special group of minerals. Many come from deep in the Earth. Some have been pushed up to the surface of the Earth by volcanoes.

Gemstones are taken out of rocks through mining. They are washed and polished. Facets are cut into them so that they can reflect light from their crystal patterns.

amber

sapphire

garnet crystals
on a white rock

Over a long time water from rivers and lakes changes rocks. Ice and wind also slowly change rocks and soil. These changes are called erosion and weathering.

Pollution happens when harmful things are put into the environment. We recycle materials to keep the Earth clean and protect its natural resources.

Minerals are natural resources found in rocks. Some kinds of minerals are very special. Most gemstones are special minerals. In this book you will learn how we find gemstones and why we value them.

Crystals and Gems

Minerals are made of atoms. An atom is the tiniest part of all things. Some atoms can come together to make crystals. A crystal is a group of atoms in a pattern, like eggs in an egg crate. Crystals come in different sizes. Rock salt comes in large crystals you can see.

Many gems are also large crystals. Gems that are crystals were formed underground long ago. Volcanoes and earthquakes push them to the surface. When gems reach the surface, people can find them.

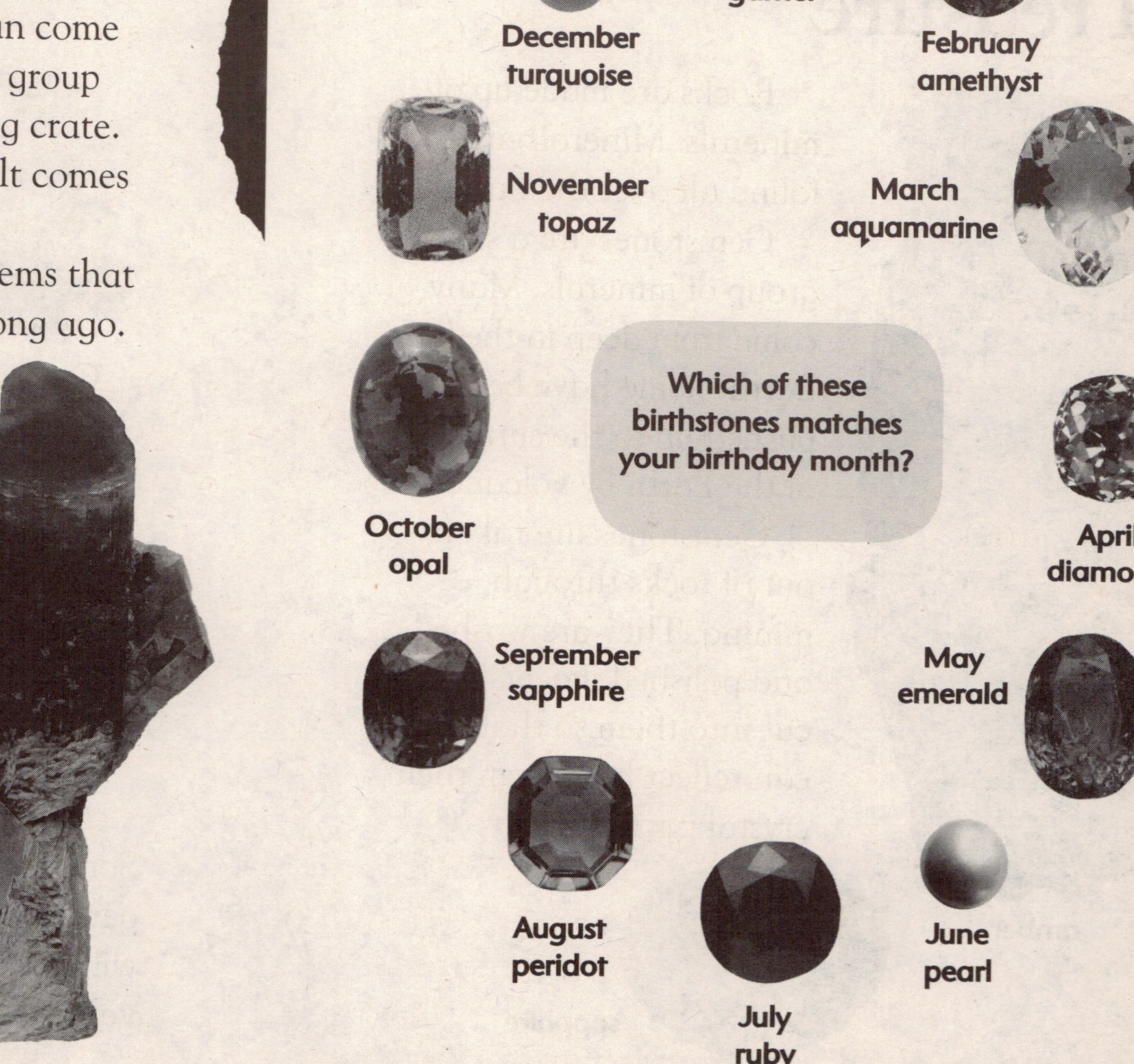

Different crystal patterns can grow next to each other.

62

Special Gems

Gemstones have been special for thousands of years. Long ago, kings and queens wore precious gems in their crowns. Pirates sometimes raided ships to steal the jewels. Many early peoples buried their rulers along with precious gems. Today, you can see the jewels from their tombs in many museums.

People in the past thought gems could help them. Emeralds were worn to protect people from animal bites. Topaz was thought to bring friends. Rubies were worn to protect people from feeling sad.

Many people still like to give gemstones as gifts for special celebrations. In many countries in the world, people give each other a ring with a gemstone when they get married. People also give gemstones as birthday gifts. Did you know there is a special list of gemstones for each month of the year? These are called birthstones.

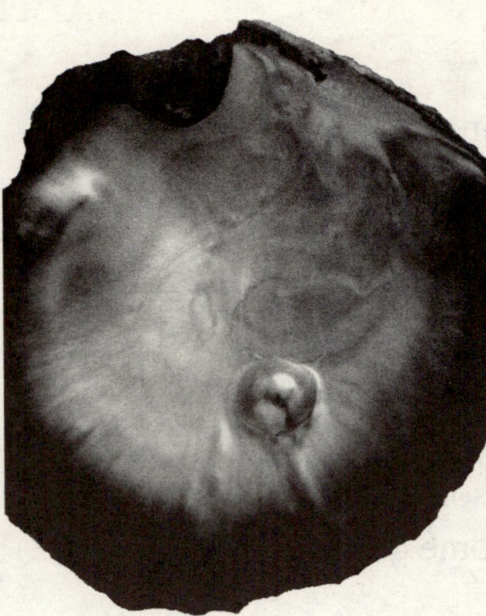
Pearls grow inside oyster shells.

pearls

Not all gems come from the Earth. Pearls grow inside oyster shells. They are shiny and beautiful when they come from the oyster. Most gemstones have to be cut by experts.

Gem cutters can make tiny rainbows of light bounce off a gem. The crystal patterns in the gem make the light do this.

Diamonds can be found under the ground.
People mine diamonds in many countries in
the world.

Sometimes miners find diamond ore along
rivers in sand and gravel. They use small pans
and water to collect diamonds. It takes sharp
eyes to tell which stones are the diamonds!
Diamond stones have to be sorted, polished,
and cut before they can become gems.

**a diamond mine
in South Africa**

Jet

Jet is also different from many other gems.
It is sometimes called black amber. Jet is not
made from crystals. It comes from ancient
plant parts. Some jet used to be wood! Millions
of years of pressure under the Earth changed
the wood into a black mineral. Like amber,
jet can be easily polished.

Jet is mined in Spain,
France, and Germany.
It is also found in Russia
and the United States.
Shiny, black stones in
jewelry are often pieces
of jet.

jet earrings

64

**Look for the
wood grain in
this piece of jet.**

Amber

Amber is different from many other gems. It is not made of crystals. Amber is made of resin, or sap, from ancient trees. Soft tree resin takes millions of years to turn into hard amber. Most amber is yellow or brown. Amber can also be red, green, or blue.

A piece of amber is very light. It is often transparent. You can sometimes see insects, leaves, or moss trapped inside. Scientists study animals and plants trapped in amber to learn about life long ago.

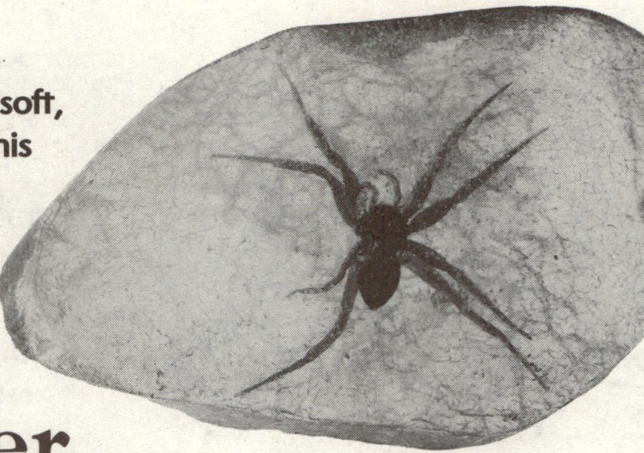

amber beads

Gems can be precious or semiprecious. Gems that are hard to find or collect are called precious. Gems that are easier to find are called semiprecious.

Scientists can also make synthetic gems. These are copies that look like real gems. Scientists grow crystals in a special container. Then they heat and apply pressure to the crystals. People buy synthetic gems because they cost less than real ones.

Synthetic gems look just like real gems.

synthetic ruby crystal

synthetic cut ruby

How hard are minerals?

Minerals can be hard or soft. Chalk is a soft mineral. You can scratch chalk with your fingernail and leave a mark. Soft minerals break into pieces. Their atoms link lightly together.

Diamonds are the hardest mineral. They have atoms made of carbon. The atoms in a diamond link together like a tight web. A diamond is strong enough to cut through other rocks. People use diamonds in cutting tools.

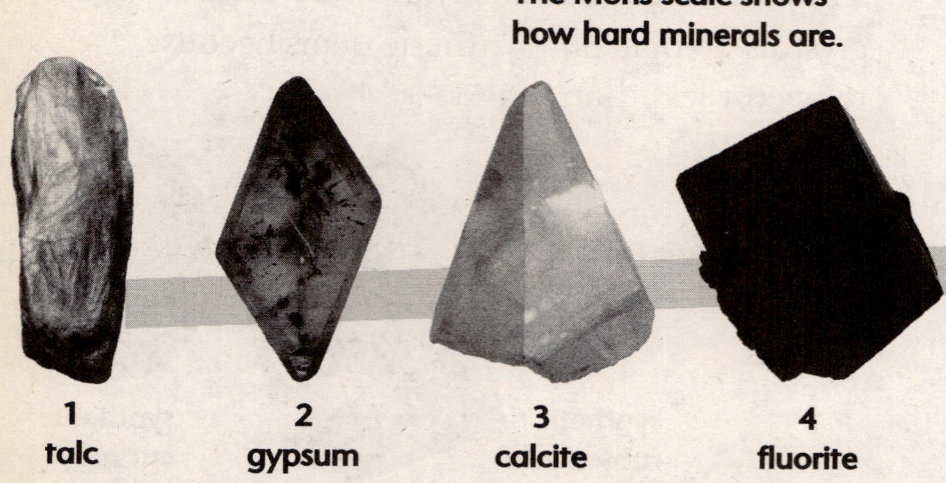

The Mohs scale shows how hard minerals are.

1 talc   **2** gypsum   **3** calcite   **4** fluorite

Uncut moonstone reflects silver, blue, and orange.

Moonstone

When light reflects off moonstone, it glows like light from the Moon. Moonstone is made from a mineral called feldspar. Half of all the rocks on Earth are made of feldspar.

Moonstones are found in several countries. Many are mined in Sri Lanka and Tanzania. They are also found in the United States.

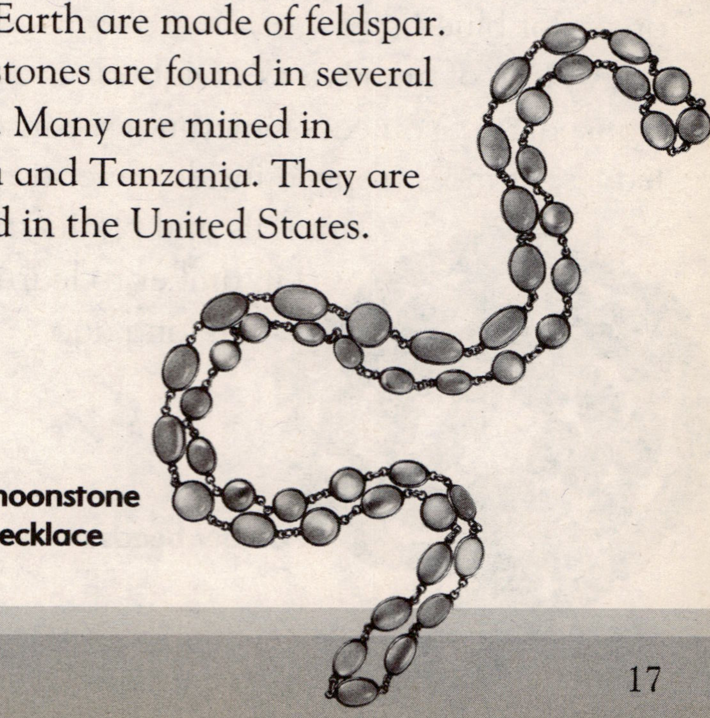

moonstone necklace

Topaz

Another gemstone made from tiny crystals is topaz. It comes in many pale colors. Topaz can be brown, blue, or green. Some topaz is red. It can also be colorless.

Topaz is a hard mineral. It can be cut into many interesting shapes. Topaz is a semiprecious gem. It is often used for rings and other jewelry.

Topaz is found in Russia, Brazil, and Australia. It is also mined in Mexico and the United States.

topaz ring

This topaz has many flaws at the bottom.

Frederick Mohs was a scientist from Germany. In 1822 he found a way to show how hard different minerals are. He gave minerals different numbers depending on their hardness. This is called the Mohs scale.

Look at the scale below. Soft minerals have low numbers. Talc is very soft. It is number 1 on the scale. Hard minerals get high numbers. Diamonds are number 10.

This rock from a volcano has a diamond in it.

diamond ring

Diamond

Diamonds were formed deep in the Earth many years ago. Diamonds need to be dug or blasted out of the ground. One of the most famous diamond mines is in South Africa.

Diamond ore is loaded into trucks and taken to a crusher. Crushed ore is then taken to be washed. Diamonds are separated from the waste material. The diamonds are sorted into five thousand different kinds! They are sorted by size, shape, color, and value.

Most diamonds are clear, like glass. Some can be light yellow. Light reflects through the patterns of their crystals. That is why diamonds sparkle. Most diamonds have facets like a baseball diamond cut into them.

Emerald

Emeralds are precious gems. They are made of a mineral called beryl. It is a hard mineral with layers of crystals.

Emeralds have been valued for thousands of years. The ancient Egyptians mined emeralds and used them to make jewelry. The finest emeralds today are found in the country of Colombia, in South America. They have been mined there for more than four hundred years.

polished emerald

cut emerald

The top of this crystal is a green emerald.

Opal

Opals are made up of tiny spheres. A sphere is a shape like a ball.

One opal stone can be red, green, blue, and yellow. The colors in an opal come from flaws. A flaw is a little crack or break in the stone. It can also be a small piece of something trapped in the stone. These flaws make opals beautiful. They also make opals softer than other gems.

Opals are found in rocks. Many opals come from Australia. Some come from Nevada, in the United States.

dark opal pendant

How many colors can you see in this uncut opal?

Quartz

Quartz can be found in small streams, in rivers, and on beaches. Quartz is made of crystals and is quite hard. Many semiprecious gems are made from quartz.

Quartz can be transparent. This means you can see through it, like water. Some quartz is opaque. This means you can't see through it at all, like milk.

There are many kinds of quartz. Amethyst quartz is purple. Citrine quartz comes in shades of transparent orange. Rose quartz is pink.

quartz beads

Amethyst is a type of quartz. Can you see the patterns of the crystals?

Ruby

Rubies come in all shades of red. They are precious gemstones. Kings and queens in Europe used rubies in their crowns. Rubies are cut from a mineral called corundum. It is very hard but not as hard as a diamond.

Rubies come from mines in Asia and Africa. Some countries where they are found are Myanmar, Sri Lanka, and Thailand.

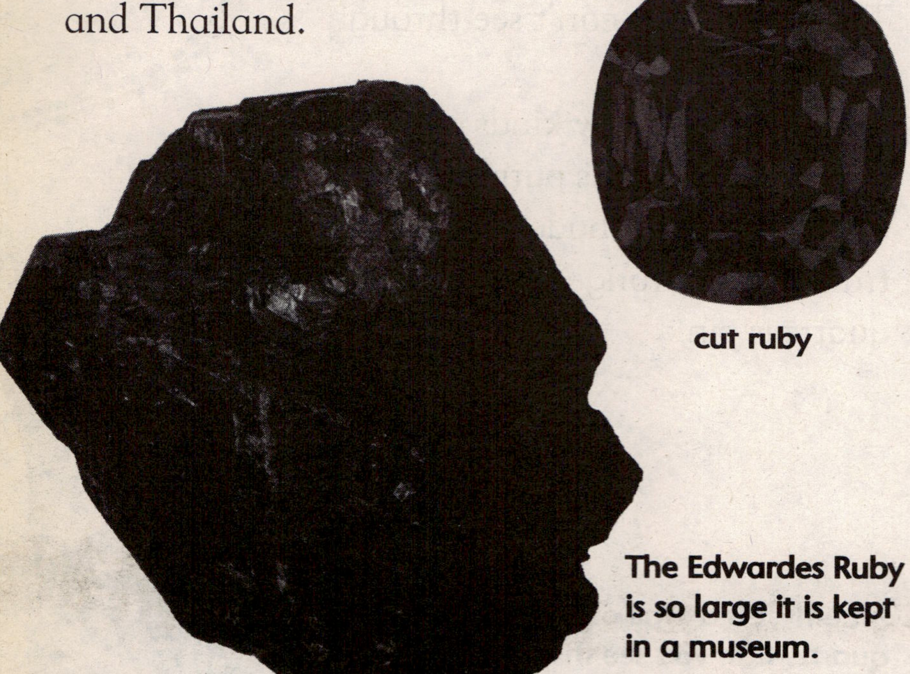
cut ruby

The Edwardes Ruby is so large it is kept in a museum.

Can you see the star in this sapphire?

sapphire in rock

Sapphire

Sapphires are precious gems. They can be pale blue or almost black. Sapphires are a hard, transparent stone. Just like rubies, they are made of corundum.

Sapphires are found in Asia. They are mined in Thailand, India, Sri Lanka, and Myanmar. They are also found in Australia. In the United States sapphires have been found in the state of Montana.

Science

Science

How Clouds Are Made

by Marilyn Greco

71

Genre	Comprehension Skill	Text Features	Science Content
Nonfiction	Draw Conclusions	• Captions • Diagrams • Glossary	Weather

Scott Foresman Science 2.6

PEARSON
Scott Foresman

DK

scottforesman.com

ISBN 0-328-13786-3

90000

9 780328 137862

What did you learn?

1. What are the three main types of cloud?

2. How do rain clouds form?

3. **Writing** in Science Snow and hail are alike in some ways and different in others. Write to explain how they are alike and how they are different. Use words from the book as you write.

4. **Draw Conclusions** How might a scientist name a cloud that was thin and wispy and low in the sky?

Picture Credits
Every effort has been made to secure permission and provide appropriate credit for photographic material.
The publisher deeply regrets any omission and pledges to correct errors called to its attention in subsequent editions.

Photo locators denoted as follows: Top (T), Center (C), Bottom (B), Left (L), Right (R), Background (Bkgd).

16 (TR) Ted Kinsman/Photo Researchers, Inc., (B) Clyde H. Smith/Peter Arnold, Inc.; 17 Gene Moore/Alamy Images;
18 John Cancalosi/Nature Picture Library.

Unless otherwise acknowledged, all photographs are the copyright © of Dorling Kindersley, a division of Pearson.

ISBN: 0-328-13786-3

Glossary

altitude	how high something is above sea level
attach	to stick to something
continuous	going on all the time
precipitation	water that falls from the sky in the form of rain, snow, sleet, or hail
predict	to tell what will happen in the future
water vapor	water in its gas form

How Clouds Are Made

by Marilyn Greco

What You Already Know

The water cycle is an important part of life on Earth. The Sun makes water on Earth evaporate. Water vapor moves up into the sky. When the water vapor gets cold, it condenses. It changes back into drops of water. The tiny drops of water form clouds. Water falls from the clouds as rain, snow, or hail. It flows into rivers, lakes, and oceans. Then the water cycle begins again.

Weather changes with the seasons. In the spring, the days can be cool or warm. Plants can grow in the spring if there is enough rain.

In summer, the days can be long and sunny. In fall, the days begin to get shorter and cooler. Some animals migrate to warmer places. In winter, the days can be very cold. Some animals hibernate, or sleep, during winter.

Fast-flowing rivers take water back to the sea.

Watching clouds can be fun. Dark, gray clouds might mean rain. Fluffy clouds might mean good weather. Next time you are outside, observe the sky carefully. You might be able to predict the weather using the clouds!

Amazing Clouds

Clouds are amazing. They change all the time. They help us know what kind of weather is coming our way. Scientists study the clouds to predict the weather.

Clouds are a part of the water cycle. They form when water vapor in the air condenses. Stratus clouds stretch out in layers. Cumulus clouds bunch together like fluff. Cirrus clouds are high, thin wisps of white. Cumulonimbus storm clouds are shaped like mushrooms.

Scientists name clouds by their shape. They also name them by their altitude.

cloudy sky

Wet weather can be dangerous. Lightning, hurricanes, and tornadoes can cause harm. Dry weather can also be dangerous. Too little rain is called a drought. Droughts can harm living things too.

Some scientists watch clouds to understand the weather. Clouds are like clues. They can show what will happen next. Read on to learn how!

Dew usually happens at night. Dew forms when air close to the ground cools off quickly. Water vapor in the air condenses into small drops of water. The drops stay on plants and other objects.

Frost may form when the ground temperature is freezing. Dew drops in the air turn into ice crystals. Frost sometimes makes beautiful shapes.

dew drops on a spiderweb

Frost is frozen dew.

Fog, Mist, and Dew

Fog, mist, and dew form when water in the air condenses near the ground. Mist is air filled with tiny droplets of water. Being in the mist is like being in a cloud right above the ground. When mist gets very thick, it is called fog. Mist and fog disappear when sunshine heats up the ground and the air. The water droplets evaporate and move higher up into the sky.

Fog is like a low-level cloud.

Clouds And The Weather

Have you ever looked up at the sky and watched the clouds? What did you see? Did you see a blue sky filled with puffy, white clouds? Did you see a sky that looked dark and gray?

Clouds come in many sizes, shapes, and colors. The sizes, shapes, and colors of clouds are always changing. No two clouds are ever exactly alike.

Just what is a cloud? A cloud is made up of many tiny drops of water stuck together. Clouds float high in the sky.

We can learn a lot by looking at clouds. Clouds can help tell us if the day will be rainy, clear, windy, or stormy. Pay attention to the clouds. Read the information they hold!

Types of Clouds

There are three main shapes of clouds: stratus, cumulus, and cirrus.

Stratus clouds are formed in flat layers. They are low in the sky. When we see stratus clouds, it can mean that a gray and dreary day lies ahead.

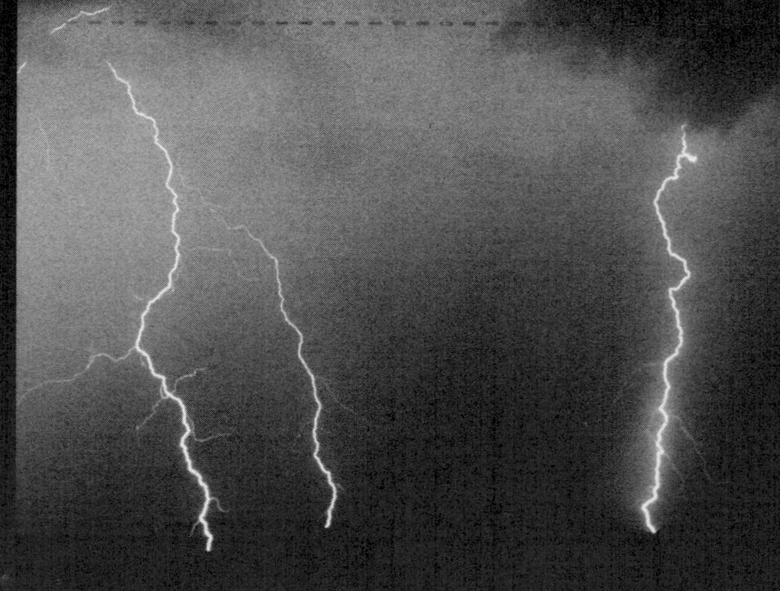

Lightning happens in storm clouds such as cumulonimbus.

Ice crystals and water droplets crash into each other. This makes static electricity. The electricity causes bright sparks to light up the sky. This is lightning.

Lightning is very, very hot. The heat from the lightning causes the air to move so fast that it makes a very loud smacking sound. This is thunder.

stratus

cumulus

Cumulus (KYOO-myoo-luhs) clouds are puffy. They can be gray or white. White cumulus clouds in a bright blue sky often mean fair weather.

Cirrus (SIR-uhs) clouds are thin and wispy. They are high in the sky. Cirrus clouds are made of tiny ice particles. But these clouds almost never make rain or snow.

Storm Clouds

Thunder and lightning can begin in storm clouds. A storm cloud, such as a cumulonimbus, happens when warm air rises quickly and moves high into the sky. When it meets colder air, the water vapor condenses.

The cloud stops moving upward. It spreads out into a shape that looks like a mushroom. It is wide at the top and narrow at the bottom. At the top of the storm cloud, water droplets turn into ice crystals. They become heavy and start to fall.

79

Clouds can be a combination of stratus,
cumulus, and cirrus. Scientists give these clouds
special names.

The first part of the name usually tells about
the cloud's altitude, or how high it is in the sky.
The second part tells about its shape. Cloud names
that begin with *strato* are low clouds. Those that
begin with *alto* are at the middle level of the sky.
Clouds names that start with *cirro* are very high.

Stratocumulus clouds are found low in the sky.
They are large and puffy. They can make light
rain or snow.

stratocumulus   cumulonimbus

**Hailstones can be as small as a pea
or as large as a softball!**

Hailstones are also made of ice, but they
form when the weather is warm. Hail forms
during thunderstorms.

A hailstone starts out as a tiny frozen water
droplet in a cumulonimbus cloud. Strong winds
toss the ice up and down. The ice crashes into
other ice crystals and water droplets.

With each toss, another layer of water
freezes onto the hailstone. It grows larger and
larger. If the wind is strong it can keep tossing
the hailstone for a long time. Finally, when the
hailstone gets very heavy, it falls to the ground.

Snow and Hail

snow crystal

When the air in a cloud
is freezing, water droplets turn into
ice crystals. More and more ice crystals stick
together. The crystals grow. When the crystals
become too heavy to remain in the air, they
start to fall.

If the air under the cloud is colder than
freezing, the crystals turn into snow. Snowflakes
are crystals of ice. Snowflakes can only happen
when the weather is cold.

Cumulonimbus clouds can be thick and dark.
Nimbus means "cloud." Cumulonimbus clouds
bring heavy rain with thunder and lightning,
hail, or snow.

Altocumulus clouds are also puffy. They can
be gray or white. They are found in the middle
level of the sky. When you see these clouds,
a thunderstorm may be coming.

Cirrocumulus clouds are fluffy and white.
They are formed in strong winds high up in the
sky. These clouds can happen when the weather
is changing.

altocumulus

cirrocumulus

The Water Cycle

Water moves between the land, the air, and the oceans. It evaporates from lakes, rivers, and plants. It forms clouds. Days later, the water falls back to the land as rain, sleet, snow, or hail. This continuous movement of water is called the water cycle.

2. The warm air rises and cools. Water vapor in the air condenses. It changes into tiny water drops or ice crystals. These form clouds.

1. The Sun warms the water and the air. The water evaporates, or changes, into water vapor.

Nimbostratus clouds look like a dark blanket across the sky.

Rain Clouds

Precipitation is the name scientists use for water that falls from clouds. Rain, snow, and hail are kinds of precipitation.

Clouds are made of tiny water droplets. As clouds grow bigger, they get heavier. Soon the drops can no longer float. They fall down to the ground. This is how rain happens.

Rain can be a light drizzle or a steady shower. Rain can be a heavy downpour.

Different kinds of clouds bring different kinds of rain. Cumulonimbus clouds bring heavy rain. Nimbostratus clouds bring light rain.

In North America, we can see rain clouds during every season of the year. However, most rain clouds happen during spring and summer.

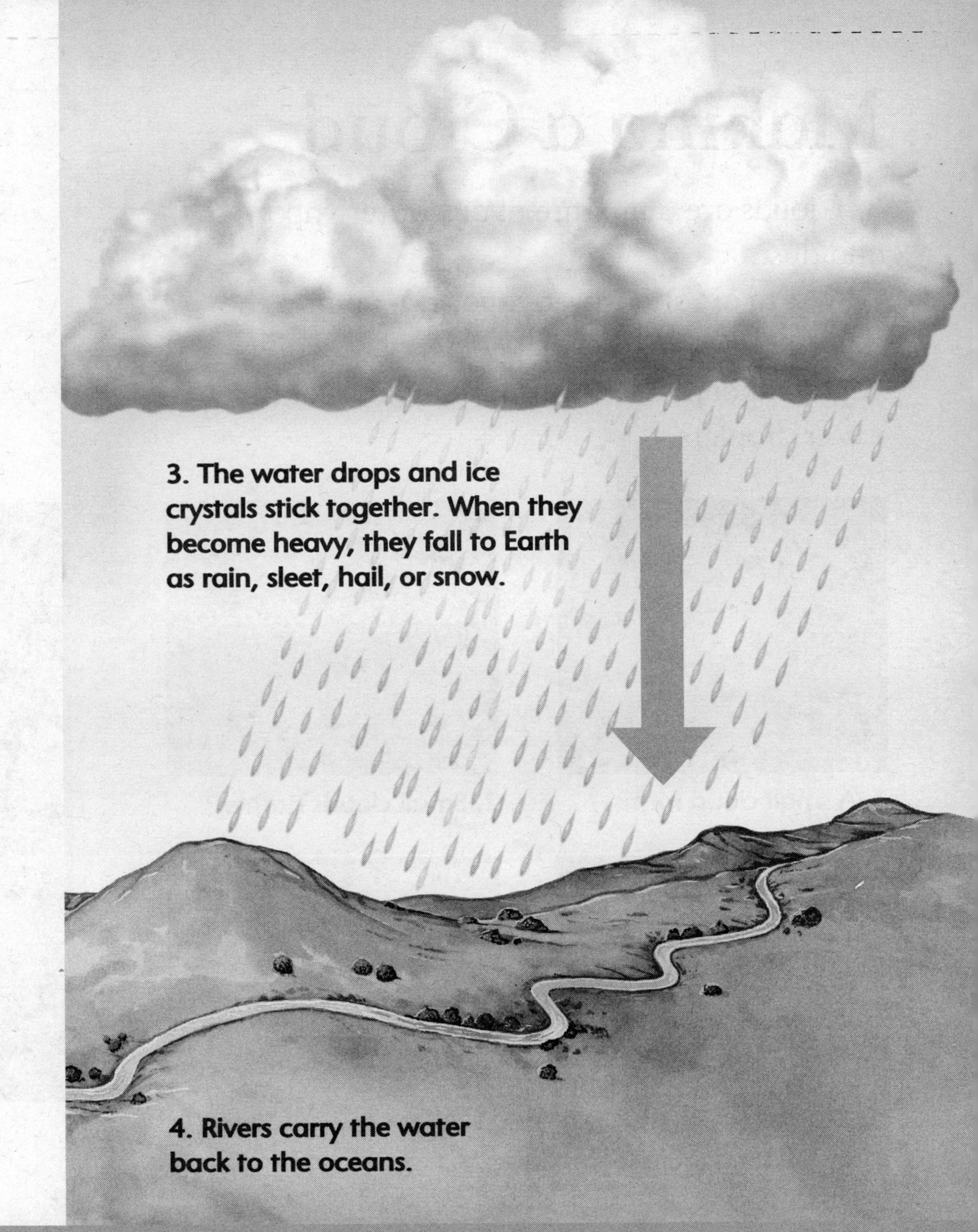

Making a Cloud

Clouds are a mixture of air, water vapor, and dust.

Warm air and water vapor rise up into the sky. As they rise, they get colder. The water vapor condenses. It turns into millions of tiny water droplets.

The water droplets stick to tiny particles of dust. Many of the droplets stick together to form a small cloud. A small cloud is light. It floats in the sky.

More and more droplets attach to each other. Small clouds join together. Soon a big, heavy cloud is made.

1. A small cloud forms.

2. Small clouds gather.

3. Small clouds join together.

4. A large cloud builds up.

5. Clouds can grow large and heavy. Rain, snow, or hail falls from heavy clouds.

Tyrannosaurus Rex

by Susan Jones Leeming

Genre	Comprehension Skill	Text Features	Science Content
Nonfiction	Retell	• Captions • Labels • Glossary	Fossils and Dinosaurs

Scott Foresman Science 2.7

PEARSON
Scott Foresman
scottforesman.com

DK

ISBN 0-328-13789-8

9 780328 137893   90000

85

Vocabulary

dinosaur
fossil
extinct
paleontologist

Extended Vocabulary

anatomy
computer animation
 models
continents
Cretaceous period
dung
excavate
scavenger

What did you learn?

1. What is the Cretaceous period?

2. Why did T. rex have a lot of holes in its skull?

3. **Writing** in Science Scientists changed their ideas about how T. rex moved. Write to explain what scientists used to think and what they think now. What made them change their minds?

4. **Retell** Some scientists think that T. rex was a hunter and some think he was a scavenger. In your own words tell what clues we have about how T. rex got its food. Use the information on pages 12–13 to help you.

Picture Credits
Every effort has been made to secure permission and provide appropriate credit for photographic material.
The publisher deeply regrets any omission and pledges to correct errors called to its attention in subsequent editions.

Photo locators denoted as follows: Top (T), Center (C), Bottom (B), Left (L), Right (R), Background (Bkgd).

6 (BL) Bettmann/Corbis; 7 (B) Bettmann/Corbis.

Scott Foresman/Dorling Kindersley would also like to thank: 5 (BL) Stephen Oliver/DK Images.

Unless otherwise acknowledged, all photographs are the copyright © of Dorling Kindersley, a division of Pearson.

ISBN: 0-328-13789-8

Glossary

anatomy	how an animal's body looks and moves
computer animation models	computer images of how animals move
continents	seven great areas of land on Earth
Cretaceous period	the time when T. rex lived
dung	animal waste
excavate	to dig up and remove from the ground
scavenger	an animal that finds and eats leftover parts of dead animals

Tyrannosaurus Rex

by Susan Jones Leeming

What You Already Know

Fossils are the remains of plants or animals that lived long ago. A fossil can look like an animal footprint or a print of a leaf. Some animal fossils come from old bones or other animal parts. They were made after an animal died and got covered by layers of mud. Over thousands of years the mud turned to stone. The shape of the animal got left in the stone.

Paleontologists study fossils to find out about animals that are extinct, or that are no longer living on Earth. Dinosaurs are extinct animals. Paleontologists study their fossil remains to learn about them. Through studying fossils, paleontologists get ideas about how dinosaurs looked and what they ate.

ammonite fossil

Dinosaur Mysteries

T. rex is one of the most interesting and amazing animals that ever lived. Paleontologists still want to know more about this "king of lizards." Perhaps scientists will discover new fossils that will help us learn more. Perhaps they will find new ways to study fossils. Maybe we will find out for sure if T. rex was a hunter or a scavenger. Until then, many people will ask questions about this mysterious giant. What questions do you have?

Although scientists may not agree on how
T. rex ate, they do agree on what it ate. Fossils
of dinosaur dung show that T. rex ate mostly
smaller, plant-eating dinosaurs. It also may have
eaten a large dinosaur called Triceratops.
Triceratops was a plant eater, but it had sharp
horns and thick skin. Triceratops must have
been hard to catch and eat, even for T. rex
with its powerful jaws!

T. rex probably ate slow-
moving duck-billed dinosaurs.

Paleontologists learn new things when they
find new fossils. Not too long ago they made a
new discovery about a dinosaur called Oviraptor.
Paleontologists thought they had found a fossil
of an Oviraptor stealing and eating eggs. Now
they know the eggs were the Oviraptors' own.

In this book, you will
read about some other
dinosaur discoveries.
You will learn what
paleontologists have
discovered about
a dinosaur called
Tyrannosaurus rex.

Tyrannosaurus rex

Who was T. rex?

Tyrannosaurus rex, or T. rex for short, is one of the most famous dinosaurs to walk the Earth. Tyrannosaurus rex is a Latin name. It means "tyrant king lizard."

T. rex is one of the largest meat-eating animals ever to have lived. It could grow as long as a large fire truck and as heavy as three cars. T. rex was tall enough to see over the top of an elephant!

Other scientists think that T. rex was a scavenger. They think its eyes were too small to see well. They think T. rex was too heavy to run fast. These scientists also think that T. rex used a large part of its brain for smelling. Scavengers need to be able to smell dead animals from very far away.

In truth, T. rex was probably both a hunter and a scavenger. It used its eyes and powerful jaws to hunt and kill smaller animals. It may also have used its sense of smell to find dead dinosaurs to scavenge.

Hunter or scavenger?

A hunter is an animal that eats other animals it catches. A scavenger is an animal that eats the leftover parts of animals caught by others.

Many scientists think T. rex was mostly a hunter. They think that T. rex used its strong back legs to chase other animals. They think it killed its prey with its powerful jaws. Animals that hunt need to have good eyes. Some scientists think that T. rex could see very well.

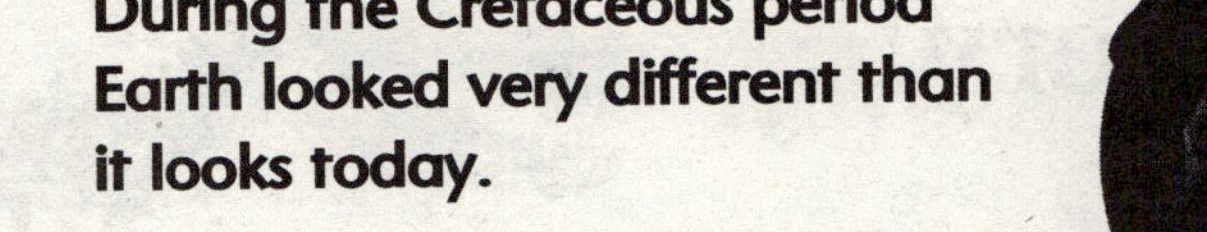

This giant lived at the end of the Cretaceous (kri-TAY-shuhs) period. This is what scientists call the time when dinosaurs such as T. rex lived. The Cretaceous period was the time between 135 million and 70 million years ago.

Scientists believe that Earth changed a lot during the Cretaceous period. The Earth's continents moved and changed shape. At the end of the Cretaceous period, dinosaurs became extinct.

Discovery!

T. rex became extinct at the end of the Cretaceous period, but some T. rex bodies got buried under sand and mud. Their skeletons slowly turned into fossils.

Barnum Brown was one of the first scientists to study dinosaurs. In 1902 he found some fossils in Montana, U.S.A. It was hard to excavate the fossils, as they were buried in rock. The fossils turned out to be the bones of a T. rex skeleton!

After the scientists dug out the fossil bones, they moved them to a museum in New York. Scientists at the museum studied the fossils. They rebuilt the T. rex skeleton.

Barnum Brown, a scientist, discovered T. rex fossils in 1902.

T. rex had very powerful jaws. A T. rex could have swallowed a human being whole! Its teeth had saw-like edges. These teeth left marks in the bones of the animals it ate. Scientists can use these bones to figure out what T. rex ate.

Each T. rex tooth was at least seven inches long. This is about as long as your forearm! With jaws and teeth like that, T. rex could easily eat other animals.

fossil of a T. rex tooth

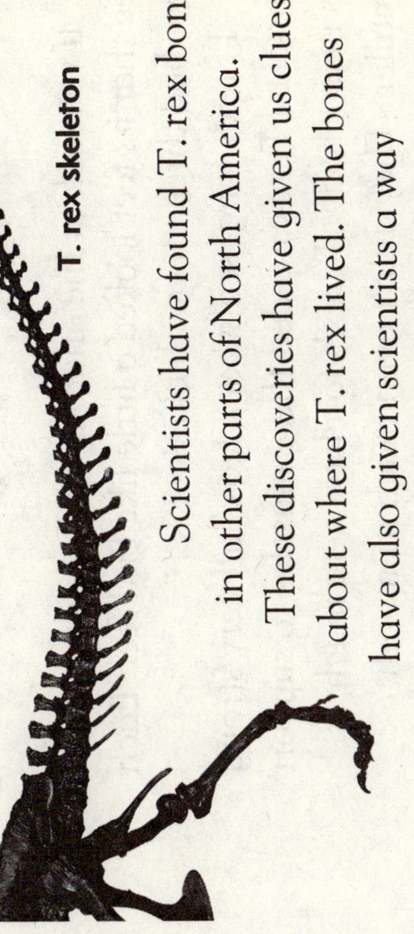

T. rex skeleton

Scientists have found T. rex bones in other parts of North America. These discoveries have given us clues about where T. rex lived. The bones have also given scientists a way to study T. rex's anatomy. An animal's anatomy is how its body looks and works.

excavation of T. rex at Hell Creek, Montana

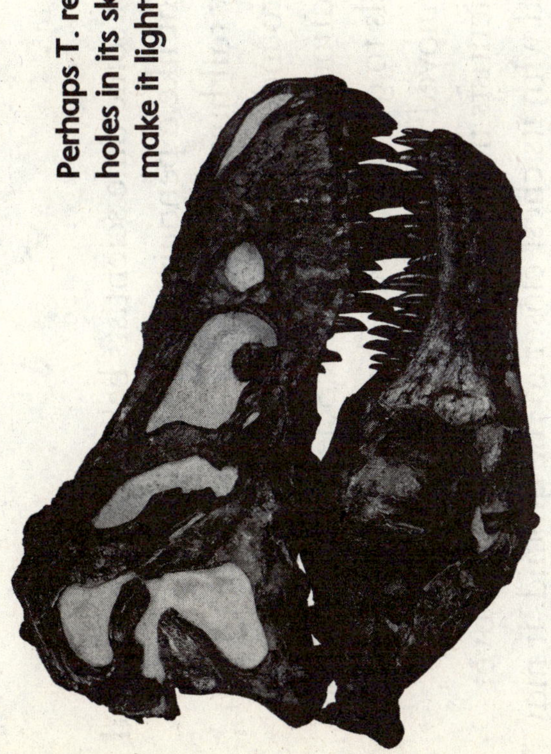

Perhaps T. rex had holes in its skull to make it lighter.

T. rex had a very heavy skull. Fossil T. rex skulls have large and small holes. Some of these holes were for its eyes and ears. Scientists think that some of the holes were empty space to make the skull lighter.

When you see how large T. rex was, its brain seems tiny! But T. rex's brain was bigger than those of many plant-eating dinosaurs. This may be because T. rex needed to do more thinking. Instead of just eating plants, it needed to think about how to hunt and catch its prey.

T. rex had powerful jaws filled with saw-like teeth.

T. rex Anatomy

If you look at the anatomy of T. rex, you will see that its feet looked a little like bird feet. Each foot had three toes with claws.

T. rex's long, scaly back legs had very strong muscles. T. rex needed these muscles to support its heavy body. T. rex's forelegs were much smaller! They didn't even reach its mouth.

Scientists think T. rex used its small forelegs for balance. T. rex may have used them to get up off the ground after lying down.

For some time scientists believed T. rex moved upright like a penguin. They thought its thick, heavy tail hung straight down, almost touching the ground. Now, scientists have computer animation models of T. rex. Scientists use these models to get new ideas about how T. rex might have moved.

Scientists now think that T. rex must have moved with its chest closer to the ground. It may have lifted its tail off the ground to help balance its heavy body.

T. rex's feet had three bird-like toes.

T. rex probably ran with its chest to the ground, using its tail for balance.

Physical Science

Air Is Everywhere

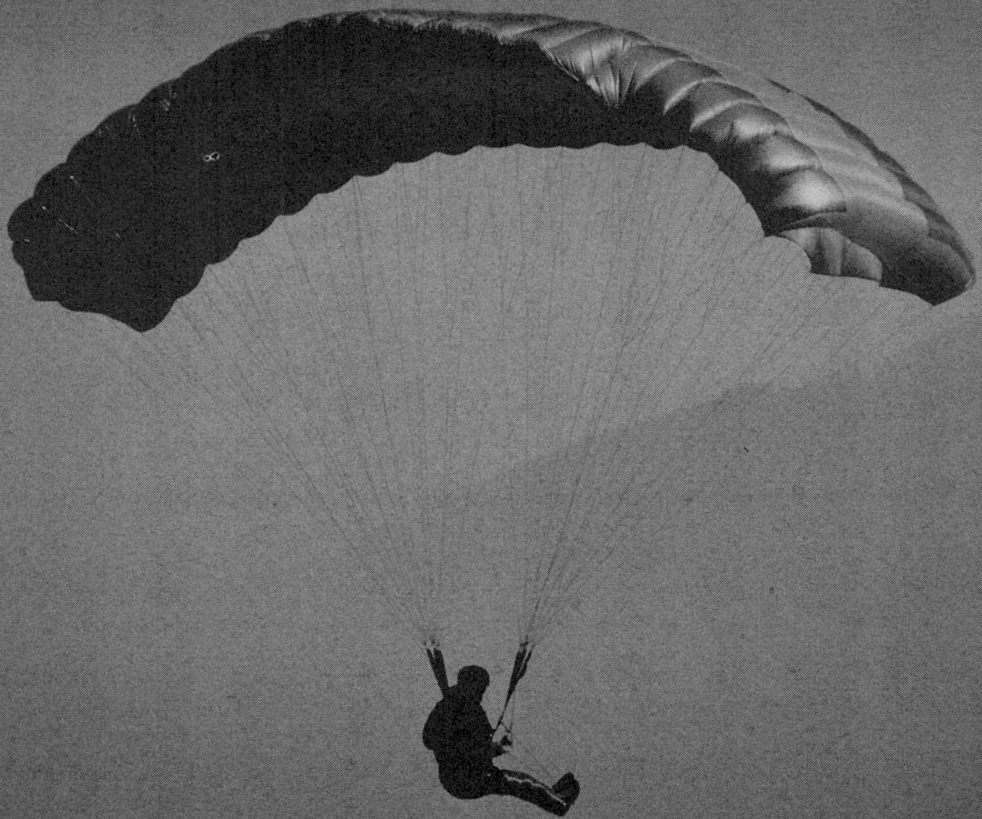

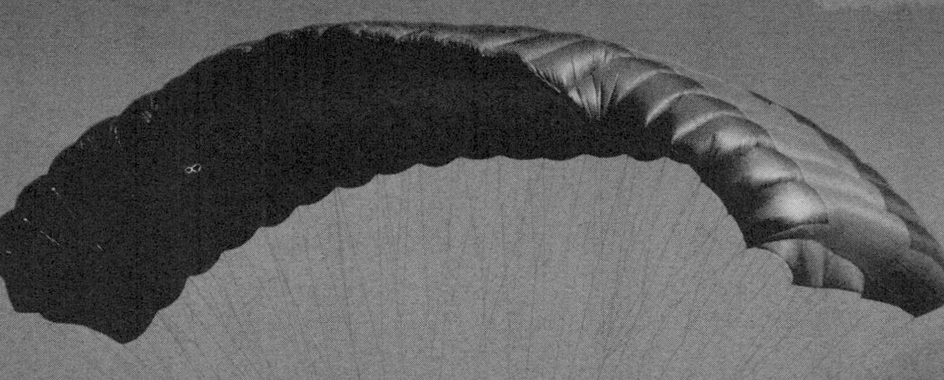

by Megan McDonald

Science

Genre	Comprehension Skill	Text Features	Science Content
Nonfiction	Draw Conclusions	• Captions • Glossary	Matter

Scott Foresman Science 2.8

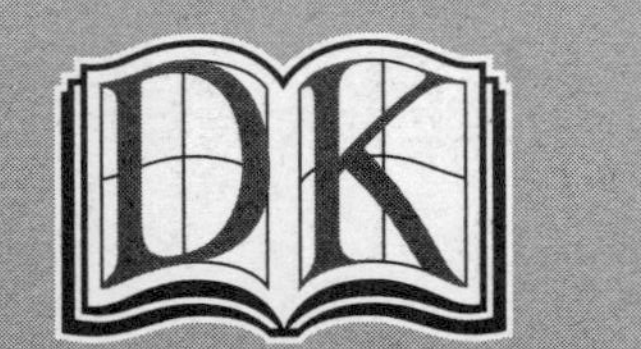

PEARSON Scott Foresman

DK

ISBN 0-328-13792-8

9 780328 137923 90000

scottforesman.com

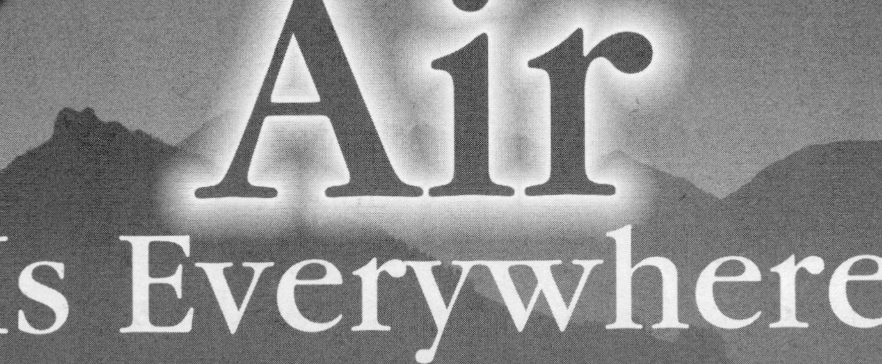

Vocabulary	Extended Vocabulary
mass	air pressure
property	air resistance
states of matter	condenses
solid	evaporates
liquid	molecules
gas	photosynthesis
mixture	precipitation

What did you learn?

1. What state of matter is air?

2. What is photosynthesis?

3. **Writing** in Science Air is important to life. Write to describe three ways in which air helps us live. Use words from the book as you write.

4. **Draw Conclusions** Why is it important for the wind to spread seeds?

Picture Credits
Every effort has been made to secure permission and provide appropriate credit for photographic material. The publisher deeply regrets any omission and pledges to correct errors called to its attention in subsequent editions.

Photo locators denoted as follows: Top (T), Center (C), Bottom (B), Left (L), Right (R), Background (Bkgd).

Opener: ©G. Kalt/Zefa/Masterfile Corporation; 10 (BR) ©Aaron Horowitz/Corbis; 15 ©Michael Howell/Index Stock Imagery; 19 Photo Library; 21 ©Jonathan Blair/Corbis; 23 ©Robert Y. Ono/Corbis.

Scott Foresman/Dorling Kindersley would also like to thank: 7 NASA/DK Images.

Unless otherwise acknowledged, all photographs are the copyright © of Dorling Kindersley, a division of Pearson.

ISBN: 0-328-13792-8

Glossary

air pressure	the pushing force made by the weight of tiny molecules of air
air resistance	the force of air slowing down objects moving through it
condenses	changes from water vapor to liquid water
evaporates	changes from a liquid into a gas
molecules	tiny, invisible particles that make up matter
photosynthesis	the process through which green plants make food in their leaves
precipitation	water that falls to the ground as rain, snow, or hail

Air
Is Everywhere

by Megan McDonald

What You Already Know

Matter is all around you. Matter is anything that takes up space and has mass. Everything that has matter has mass. Mass is the amount of matter in an object.

Different kinds of matter have different properties. A property is something about an object that you can observe with your senses. For example, the color and shape of an object are its properties.

There are three different states of matter. Matter can be a solid, liquid, or gas. A solid is matter that has its own size and shape. Solids take up space and have mass. Liquid is matter that does not have its own shape. Liquids take the shape of their containers. Liquids take up space and have mass. Gas is matter that takes the size and shape of its container. Gas has mass.

Air Is Important

Air is an important gas. Without air, we could not live. People need oxygen in the air to breathe and to get energy. Plants use carbon dioxide in the air to make their food.

Air heats up, moves, rises, and cools. It helps create clouds, rain, and wind. Some winds, such as tornadoes, can be dangerous. Wind can also be very useful. Wind can scatter seeds from plants. It can power windmills.

People use air for fun too. Hot air balloons use air to float up into the sky. Windsurfers use the wind to dart across the water. Airplanes speed through the air to bring people to faraway places.

Air is necessary for life. It is useful and fun. Look around you. Feel it on your skin. Air is everywhere.

Matter can be changed in different ways. You can change the size or shape of matter. You can also stir matter together to make a mixture. A mixture is something made up of two or more things that do not change. You can separate a mixture and see each part.

Another way to change matter is by cooling or heating it. Water is matter. You can cool water enough to turn it into ice. You can heat the ice to turn it back into liquid. You can even heat liquid water enough to turn it into gas. The water evaporates into the air.

You are about to read more about one state of matter. Air is a gas, and it is all around us.

What is air?

Air is a gas. It is all around us. Air is made up of tiny particles called molecules. We cannot see air molecules, but they take up space and have mass.

Air is touching us all the time. We cannot see air, but sometimes we can feel it. Have you ever felt the wind on your skin? That is air.

Air is springy. It pushes back when you squash it. If you squeeze air into a small space, the tiny air molecules get pushed together. The air pressure in that space gets stronger.

You can feel the pressure of air when you squeeze a ball or a bicycle tire. The air is pushed into a smaller space and feels tight. When you let go, the ball or tire will spring out again. The air molecules have pushed back.

Some machines work using high-pressure air. Some drills can even use air pressure to blast holes in concrete.

This drill uses the strong force of air under pressure.

Air Under Pressure

Tiny molecules of air that we cannot see press down on objects around them. This is called air pressure. Air molecules can cause pressure because they take up space and have weight.

Air pressure gets less strong the higher we go, because there are fewer air molecules. We are so used to the air pushing against us that we do not even feel it!

The air in these bicycle tires is under pressure.

An air-filled balloon weighs more than an empty balloon.

We can also see what air does around us. The wind can carry a kite. It can make trees sway. When you blow up a balloon, you are filling it with air. Now the balloon takes up more space and weighs more.

Air for Life

Air is important for life. Air contains oxygen. We need oxygen to breathe. Oxygen in the air helps our bodies release energy from the food we eat. The more active we are, the more oxygen we need. People need to take in a lot of air when they play sports.

Air resistance helps these parachutes fall gently to the ground.

Air resistance helps people land parachutes. It slows them down as they fall through the air. Parachutes are big pieces of cloth. They are made to catch a lot of air resistance.

Air resistance can be a problem. People do not want cars and planes to be slowed down by air. Cars and planes have special shapes so they get less air resistance.

Air Resistance

Air resistance is a force that slows down objects moving through air. You can feel air resistance when you go down a hill on your bike. It feels like the air is pushing against you.

Astronauts bring air with them to space.

Air is thinner up high. This means that there are fewer air molecules. If you climb a tall mountain, you will need to breathe faster. This happens because it is harder for you to get the air you need.

In space, there is no air at all. This is why astronauts must carry air with them. They breathe air from special tanks on their backs.

Air and Plants

Plants need air too. They use air to get energy from their food. Plants use different gases found in the air.

One of the gases they use is carbon dioxide. Plants use carbon dioxide, water, and sunlight to make food in their leaves. This is called photosynthesis.

When the clouds become heavy enough, the water falls to the ground as rain. Scientists call this precipitation.

Snow is another kind of precipitation. Water droplets in clouds turn into snowflakes when the air is below freezing. Snow has a lot of air trapped in it. This is why snow looks white.

Moisture in the Air

Air has moisture in it. This moisture is called water vapor. Water vapor is a gas. Warm air and water vapor rise. Then they cool. When air cools, the water vapor in it condenses to form clouds. Moisture from clouds is frozen when it begins to fall. If the air is warm, it changes to rain.

Rain and snow are kinds of precipitation.

Many plants also need air for another reason. The wind helps spread their seeds. Some plants, such as dandelions, have seeds that are connected to fluff. The wind carries the fluff through the air. When the wind stops blowing, the seeds fall to the ground. Then new plants can grow.

These seeds get scattered by air.

Air on the Move

Air moves all the time. Moving air is called wind. Wind is caused by different temperatures of air. Warmer, lighter air gets pushed along by cooler, heavier air. Sometimes wind can be a soft, light breeze. Sometimes it can be strong, such as a hurricane or a tornado.

Hot air balloons make use of warm, rising air.

A hot air balloon can float because it has warm air in it. The bag of air is heated by a burner under the balloon. The balloon rises until the temperature of the air inside the bag is the same as the air outside. As the air in the bag cools, the balloon slowly starts to go down. The people inside can control the balloon by warming or cooling the air.

Rising Air

Hot air is lighter than cool air. Air that is warm rises up. People can use hang gliders to soar through the air. Birds, such as eagles and sea gulls, soar on rising waves of air. The warm air keeps the birds' bodies lifted. Birds that glide have big wings so they can catch as much air as possible.

An eagle rides on a wave of warm air.

Hurricanes are storms with powerful winds. The center of a hurricane is called the hurricane's eye. The eye of a hurricane is calm. The winds around the eye are very strong. Hurricanes have winds that move more than one hundred miles per hour.

Tornadoes are twisting winds that form a funnel-shaped cloud. When this touches down, it tears up everything in its path. The winds of a tornado can reach a speed of three hundred miles per hour.

Tornadoes can be very dangerous.

Wind Power

Wind is very powerful. Sometimes, as with hurricanes and tornadoes, wind can be dangerous. Sometimes we can use the power of the wind to help us. Windmills capture energy from the wind. This energy can then be used in many ways.

People have been using windmills for centuries.

The wind blows on the blades of the windmill and spins them like a pinwheel. The turning blades, or vanes, can run machines.

People have been using windmills for hundreds of years to pump water and grind grain. Today, people use wind power to make electricity. The energy that moves through wind turbines could power whole cities.

Ships and Boats

by Marilyn Greco

Science

Science

Genre	Comprehension Skill	Text Features	Science Content
Nonfiction	Infer	• Call Outs • Captions • Glossary	Energy

Scott Foresman Science 2.9

PEARSON
Scott Foresman

DK

ISBN 0-328-13795-2

9 780328 137954

90000

scottforesman.com

What did you learn?

<table>
<tr><td>Vocabulary</td><td>Extended Vocabulary</td></tr>
<tr><td>conductor</td><td>ballast</td></tr>
<tr><td>energy</td><td>foil</td></tr>
<tr><td>fuel</td><td>harbor</td></tr>
<tr><td>reflect</td><td>hull</td></tr>
<tr><td>shadow</td><td>mast</td></tr>
<tr><td>solar energy</td><td>sail</td></tr>
<tr><td>source</td><td></td></tr>
</table>

1. How do people use ships and boats?

2. How does a ballast work?

3. **Writing** in Science People use different kinds of energy to move ships and boats through water. Write to tell about three types of fuel or energy used to move ships and boats. Use examples from the book as you write.

4. **Infer** Over time, people have discovered new forms of energy that can make boats bigger and faster. If these boats are easier to use, why do you think people still use muscle- and wind-powered boats?

Picture Credits

Every effort has been made to secure permission and provide appropriate credit for photographic material. The publisher deeply regrets any omission and pledges to correct errors called to its attention in subsequent editions.

Photo locators denoted as follows: Top (T), Center (C), Bottom (B), Left (L), Right (R), Background (Bkgd).

Opener: ©Richard Cummins/Corbis; 7 Phil Schermeister/Corbis; 11 ©Richard Cummins/Corbis; 13 Mike Segar/Reuters/Corbis; 14 Craig Aurness/Corbis; 19 Bob Rowan/Progressive Image/Corbis; 23 Richard Hamilton Smith/Corbis.

Unless otherwise acknowledged, all photographs are the copyright © of Dorling Kindersley, a division of Pearson.

ISBN: 0-328-13795-2

Ships and Boats

by Marilyn Greco

Glossary

ballast water or air to help a submarine sink or float

foil a wing-like shape on the bottom of a hydrofoil

harbor a place safe from rocks and rough winds, where a ship can reach the land

hull the body of a boat

mast a long pole that holds up a ship's sails

sail a large piece of cloth made to catch the wind

111

What You Already Know

We use energy every day. We use energy when we run, when we sleep, and when we breathe. Anything that can do work and cause change has energy.

Solar energy is heat and light from the Sun. Green plants get energy from the Sun. Animals get energy from food. People get energy from many different kinds of healthful foods.

Sunlight is a source of heat. A source is a place from which things come. Fuel is something that is burned to make heat.

Fruits and vegetables get energy from the Sun.

For thousands of years, people have used boats. The first boats were moved by muscle power. Next, wind power was used. Sailboats and sailing ships were used for travel, trade, and warfare. Then people began to use steam engines. Today, people use all kinds of boats for many purposes. Some boats are still powered by muscles or the wind. Some boats use fuels, such as gasoline.

People use boats for work and for fun. Boats are a wonderful invention.

Boats for Fun

Some kinds of boats have been invented just for fun. In the 1950s, boating became more popular. People started buying their own boats.

Some people use wind-powered boats to sail quietly. Some hold sailing races. Motorboats can be used for racing or for relaxing. They are powered by gasoline fuel.

Dinghies are powered by the wind.

Heat moves from hot places to cool places. A conductor is something that lets heat move easily through it. Metal is a good conductor of heat.

Light is a form of energy. It reflects when it bounces off something. A shadow happens when something blocks light. Other kinds of energy include motion, wind, sound, and electricity.

In this book, you will read about boats and ships. What do boats and ships have to do with energy? People use different kinds of boats. People also use different kinds of energy to move boats and ships through water.

paddles

On the Water

Have you ever been to a lake, a large river, or the seashore? If you have, you probably saw ships and boats in action.

Ships and boats come in all shapes and sizes. There are small canoes, medium-sized tugboats, and huge oil tankers. All boats, no matter what size, need energy to move through water.

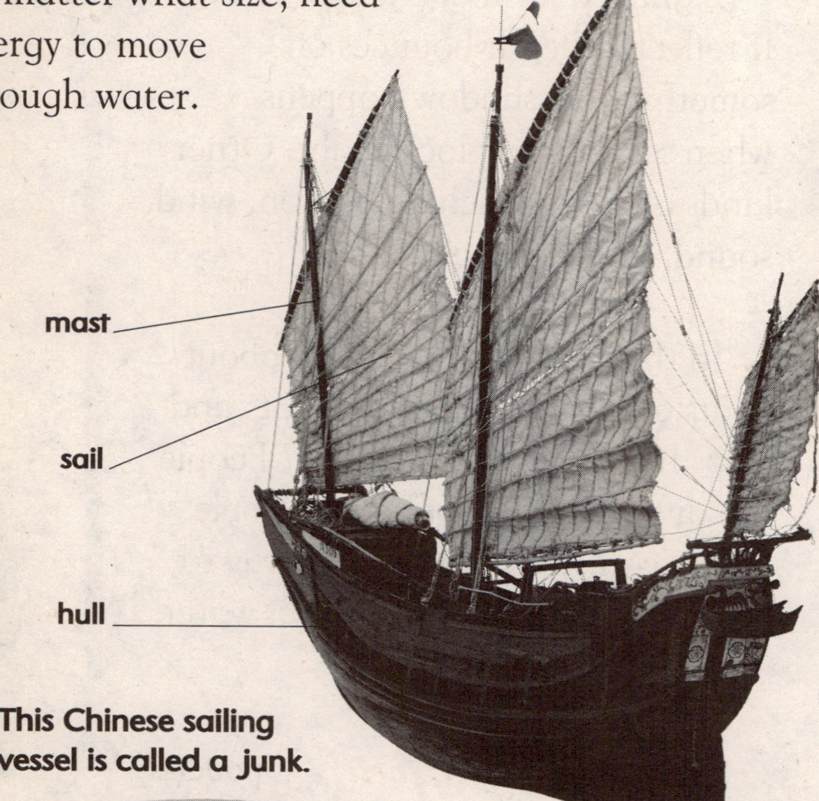

This Chinese sailing vessel is called a junk.

The *Trieste* can reach great depths in the ocean.

Some submarines are no larger than a car. People use small submarines to explore the ocean and discover how ocean plants and animals live.

Some submarines are very large. They can be twice the size of an airplane. Large submarines belong to the world's navies. Such submarines have been used to sink or destroy enemy ships. They have also been used for spying.

Under the Waves

Most ships are made to float on water. Submarines are made to sink! They travel under the water. How do submarines do this?

A submarine has ballast tanks. When the tanks are filled with air, the submarine can float. When the tanks are filled with water, the submarine can sink. When the submarine needs to come up to the surface, the water is pumped out, and the tanks are once again filled with air. Most submarines are powered by nuclear energy.

The USS *Seawolf* is a fast, quiet, and powerful navy submarine.

This cruise liner was a passenger ship. It has several decks, or levels. It carried several thousand people.

Muscle Power

People began making boats more than ten thousand years ago. At first, they made simple rafts. Then people found a new way to make boats. They carved out the trunks of trees to make long, narrow boats.

These early boats, or canoes, needed energy to push them through water. People powered these boats, using their own muscle power. People pushed with wooden poles or rowed with oars. They could use their boats to hunt, fish, and carry goods from place to place.

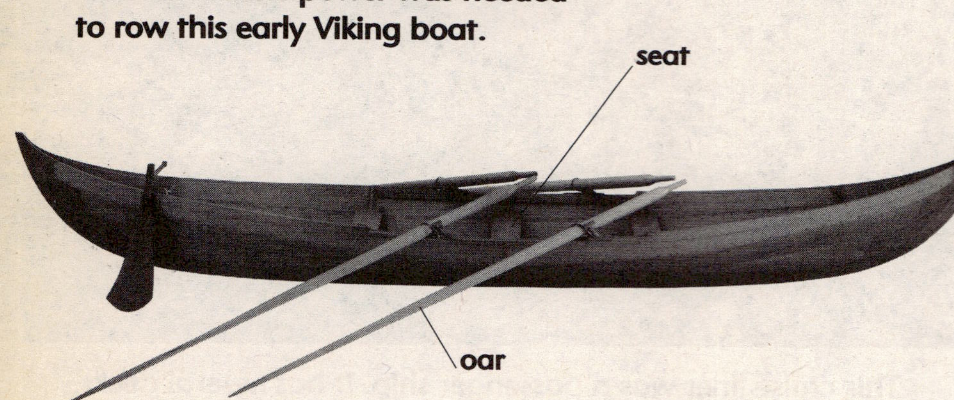

Human muscle power was needed to row this early Viking boat.

The hydrofoil has been called a flying ship.

Hydrofoils are similar to hovercrafts. They are lifted off the water by small water wings. The wings, or foils, help the ship move at great speeds. Instead of pushing lots of water out of the way, the foils only need to push a little water out of the way. Hydrofoils can move much more easily than a ship with a hull.

Above the Waves

Over time, people tried to find ways to make boats faster. They invented the hovercraft and the hydrofoil. These boats do not float in the water. Instead, they float just above the water. Usually, they use gasoline engines.

Most ships need to push water out of the way to move through it. A hovercraft blows air down onto the water. It floats above the water on this cushion of air. This way, it does not need to push water out of the way. It moves along very quickly.

The first hovercraft crossed the English Channel in 1959.

Muscle-powered boats are still used today. Some people use these boats for fun. Other people use them for work. People enjoy using canoes, rowboats, and kayaks. Sometimes fishermen use these boats. Muscle-powered boats can be used as emergency craft. They can be used by lifeguards to rescue swimmers who might need help.

Sailing Ships

As time passed, people discovered that wind power could be used to move boats. People invented sails to capture the wind. Sails are large sheets of cloth. The cloth is attached to a long pole called a mast. Sailboats can travel more easily than boats powered by muscles. Sailboats can also move more quickly than muscle-powered boats can move.

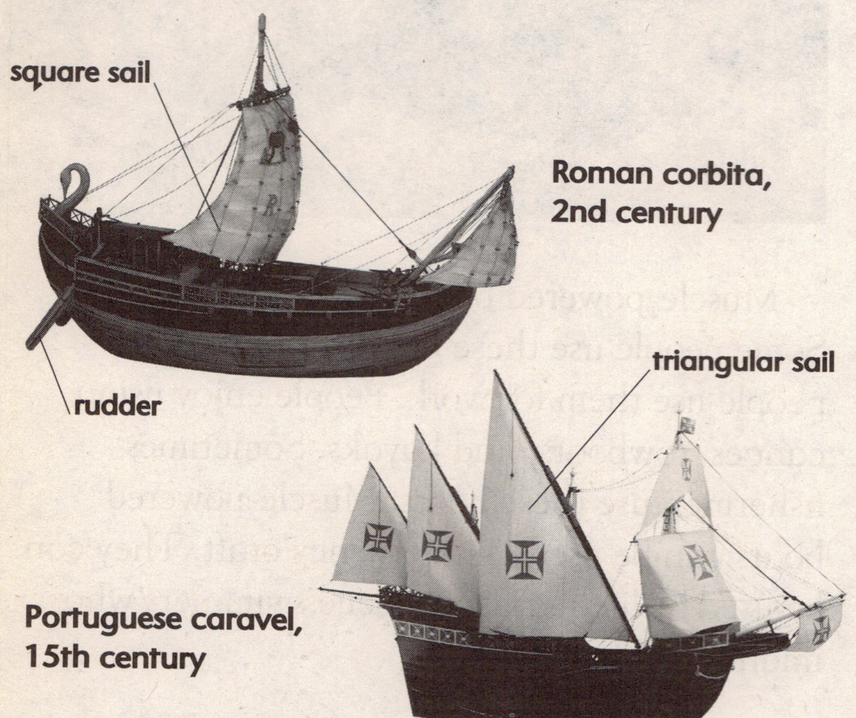

The *Bismarck* was a German warship. It was sunk during World War II by the British Royal Navy.

Battleships were used during World War II. This picture shows a famous German battleship called the *Bismarck*. This ship was sunk in 1941 after a battle that lasted many days. The wreck of the *Bismarck* was found in 1989 at the bottom of the Atlantic Ocean.

Ships at War

From early times, people have used ships in war. The ancient Greeks and Romans used warships to fight battles at sea. Today, many countries have navies. Navies have large warships.

Some warships carry soldiers and goods from place to place. Other warships carry weapons. Aircraft carriers are huge ships that carry airplanes. Airplanes can take off from and land on the decks of aircraft carriers.

Warships are powered in many ways. Steam, diesel, and nuclear power move these ships.

cargo ship, 19th century

iron hull

This ship, called the HMS *Eagle,* can carry more than sixty aircraft.

Many ancient peoples traveled using wind-powered boats. The ancient Egyptians used boats with sails. The Greeks and Romans used them too. Later, European explorers started using sailing ships to travel to other parts of the world. They also used their ships to bring back goods from faraway lands. We call the ships they used cargo ships.

119

Steamers

The steam engine was invented in the late 1700s. In the 1800s, people started using steam engines to move boats. The first steamboats used paddle wheels. These big wheels could move the boats through the water. Unlike sailboats, steamboats could move quickly without wind. They could even move against the wind.

propeller

Sometimes two or more tugboats are needed to pull a very large ship.

Tugboats are kept in large ports and harbors. Their job is to push or pull large ships. They help ships get in and out of harbors.

People use lifeboats for work too. Lifeboats are often kept on bigger ships. They are used to save people from drowning.

Some steam trawlers were used for fishing.

This lifeboat is kept on the shore.

Boats at Work

Some boats are used for work. There are many kinds of working boats. There are large oil tankers. There are strong tugboats. There are ferries. There are lifeboats. Today, most working boats use diesel fuel for power.

Oil tankers have a big job. They can carry up to 500,000 tons of crude oil. The oil is shipped to refineries all over the world. Crude oil is turned into fuel, such as gasoline. This fuel can be used for cars, boats, and airplanes.

People burned a fuel, such as coal, to boil water. This made steam. The force of the steam turned the paddle wheel. Later, people made a smaller and better kind of paddle. It was called a propeller.

Steam power changed travel. It allowed many people to travel long distances.

Paddle steamers can be found along the Mississippi River.

Oil tankers carry many tons of crude oil.

Ocean Liners

Ocean liners were built starting in the 1840s. These boats were made to carry many passengers. These ships were called liners because they had regular routes, or lines.

Ocean liners could travel long distances. They could cross the Atlantic and Pacific Oceans. They could travel from one continent to another.

These large and fast ships could carry more than a thousand people. In the 1920s and 1930s, people traveled in ocean liners for fun.

People kept building larger and faster ocean liners. In 1934, the *Queen Mary I* was built. At that time, it was the largest ship ever built. It could carry more than two thousand people.

Most ocean liners used steam engines for power. Some had diesel engines. These engines burned diesel fuel.

Magnet Fun

by Lisa Oram

Genre	Comprehension Skill	Text Features	Science Content
Nonfiction	Put Things in Order	• Captions • Glossary	Forces and Motion

Scott Foresman Science 2.10

PEARSON
Scott Foresman

DK

ISBN 0-328-13798-7

9 780328 137985

90000

scottforesman.com

Vocabulary

attract
force
friction
gravity
motion
repel
simple machine
work

Extended Vocabulary

electromagnet
lodestone
magnetic field
magnetic material
magnetism

What did you learn?

1. Is a paper napkin made of magnetic material? How can you find out?

2. What happens when you put a magnet's north pole near another magnet's north pole?

3. **Writing** in Science In this book you read about how Earth is like a magnet. In your own words explain how this works. Use words from the book as you write.

4. **Put Things in Order** List, in the correct order, the steps for making a fishing game with magnets.

Picture Credits
Every effort has been made to secure permission and provide appropriate credit for photographic material. The publisher deeply regrets any omission and pledges to correct errors called to its attention in subsequent editions.

Photo locators denoted as follows: Top (T), Center (C), Bottom (B), Left (L), Right (R), Background (Bkgd).

9 (BR) Alex Bartel/Photo Researchers, Inc.; 14 Michael S. Yamashita/Corbis.

Unless otherwise acknowledged, all photographs are the copyright © of Dorling Kindersley, a division of Pearson.

ISBN: 0-328-13798-7

Magnet Fun

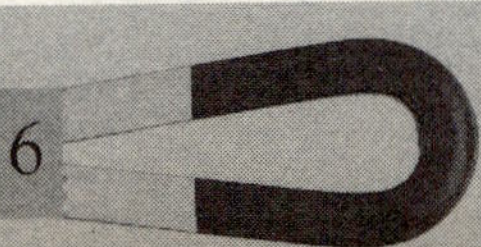

by Lisa Oram

Glossary

electromagnet	a magnet made with electricity, whose magnetic force can be turned on and off
lodestone	a natural magnetic rock made mostly of iron
magnetic field	the area around a magnet in which a magnetic force can be felt
magnetic material	an object that can stick to a magnet
magnetism	the force of a magnet

What You Already Know

Motion is the act of moving. Objects can move in different ways and in different directions. A force is a push or pull that makes an object move. It takes a lot of force to move some objects. It takes only a little force to move other objects.

Some forces do particular jobs and have special names. Gravity is a force that pulls things toward Earth. When you jump, gravity pulls you back to Earth. Using force to move an object is work. You do more work if you use a lot of force to move an object.

Many tools and machines depend on electromagnets to work. Electromagnets in the handset of this telephone allow you to hear someone else's voice. The magnetic force turns the electric signals into sounds you can hear.

Our lives would be very different without magnets. Magnets are all around us!

Even telephones use magnets to work.

Electric Magnets

Electric magnets are not like other magnets. Their magnetism comes from electricity. Electricity turns the magnetic force on and off.

A piece of iron or steel is attached to a wire that carries electricity. When the electric current comes through the wire and touches the piece of metal, the metal is magnetized.

This giant electric magnet picks up scrap metal.

Friction is a force that slows down or stops moving objects. When there is a little friction, objects will move easily. When there is a lot of friction, objects are harder to move. Friction makes heat. You can feel this when you rub your hands together.

A simple machine is a tool with few or no moving parts. A wheel and axle, a wedge, a screw, and a lever are examples of simple machines. Some animal body parts, such as a bird's beak, work like simple machines.

Magnets can push or pull certain metal objects. Attract means to pull toward. Repel means to push away. The strongest parts of a magnet are called the magnet's poles.

Magnets can be very useful, and they can also be a lot of fun. In this book, you will learn more about magnets.

What is a magnet?

There are magnets in many things around you. Some puzzles and games use magnetic pieces. Cabinet and refrigerator doors can close with magnets. Some magnets are hidden in machines, such as those inside a computer.

The force of a magnet is called magnetism. You can't see magnetism, but you can feel it.

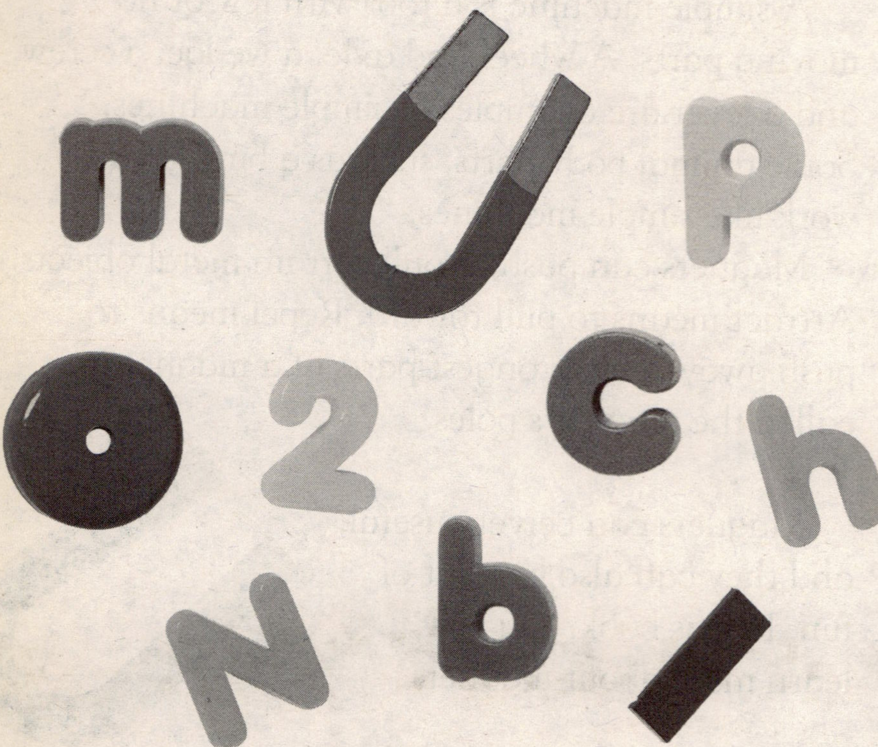

Earth's North Pole and South Pole act like the poles of a magnet.

Look at a compass. The needle in it is a magnet. It has a north and a south pole. When the needle moves, its south pole is attracted to Earth's North Pole. The south pole of the needle always points north. Once you know which way is north, you can find your way with a map.

A compass needle is a magnet. It is attracted to Earth's North Pole.

Earth's Magnetism

All of Earth is magnetic. Under the surface on which we live, most of Earth is made of iron. Earth's iron center makes Earth a magnet. A magnetic field surrounds our planet for many miles.

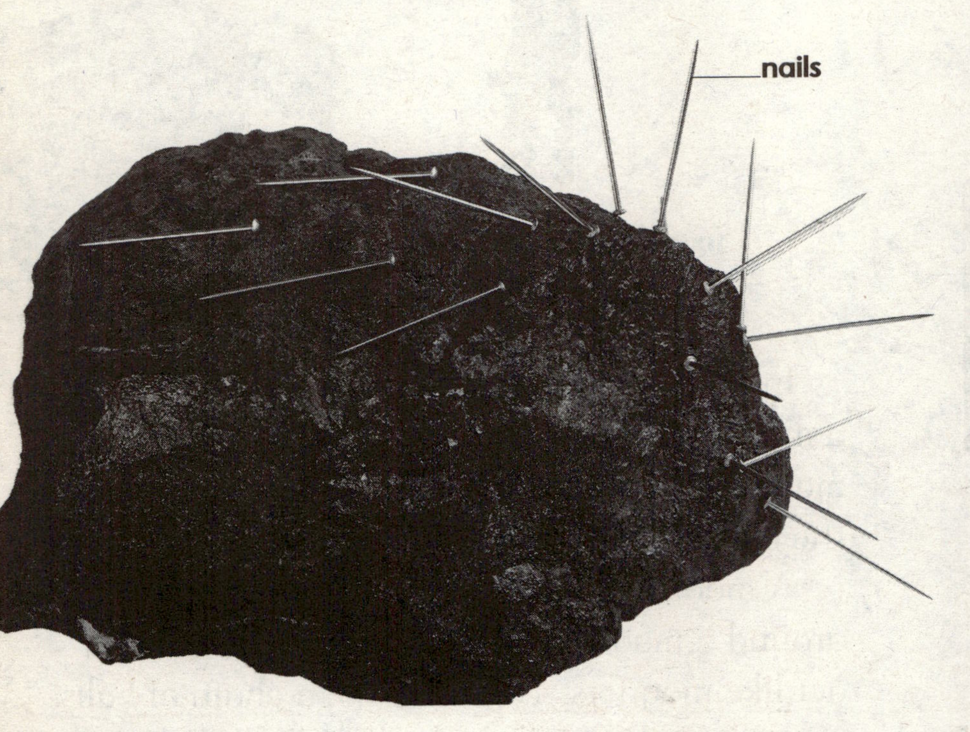

Magnetism was first discovered in a rock called lodestone. Lodestone is made mostly of iron.

Try gathering magnets together. Find ones of different sizes and shapes.

How do they act on each other? Is the magnetic force the same in all parts of a magnet? What happens if you try stacking the magnets?

Magnets have different strengths. How can you tell which ones are the strongest?

Magnets attract each other.

Magnetic Materials

Magnetic materials contain metal. This metal is usually iron. Magnetic materials stick to a magnet.

Look at the objects in the picture. Which ones are made of magnetic material?

Foil is made of metal, but it's not magnetic. Foil is made from a metal called aluminum. It does not contain iron, so it does not stick to a magnet.

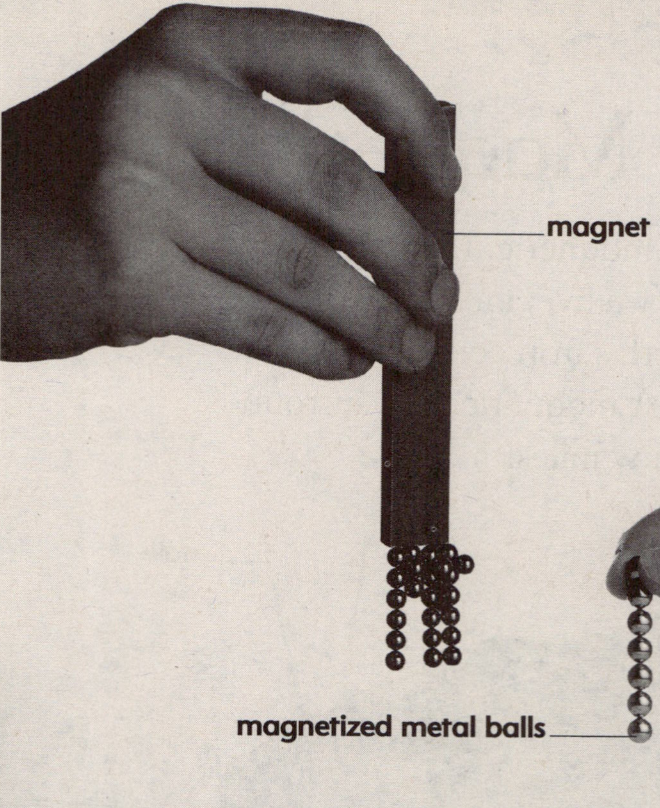

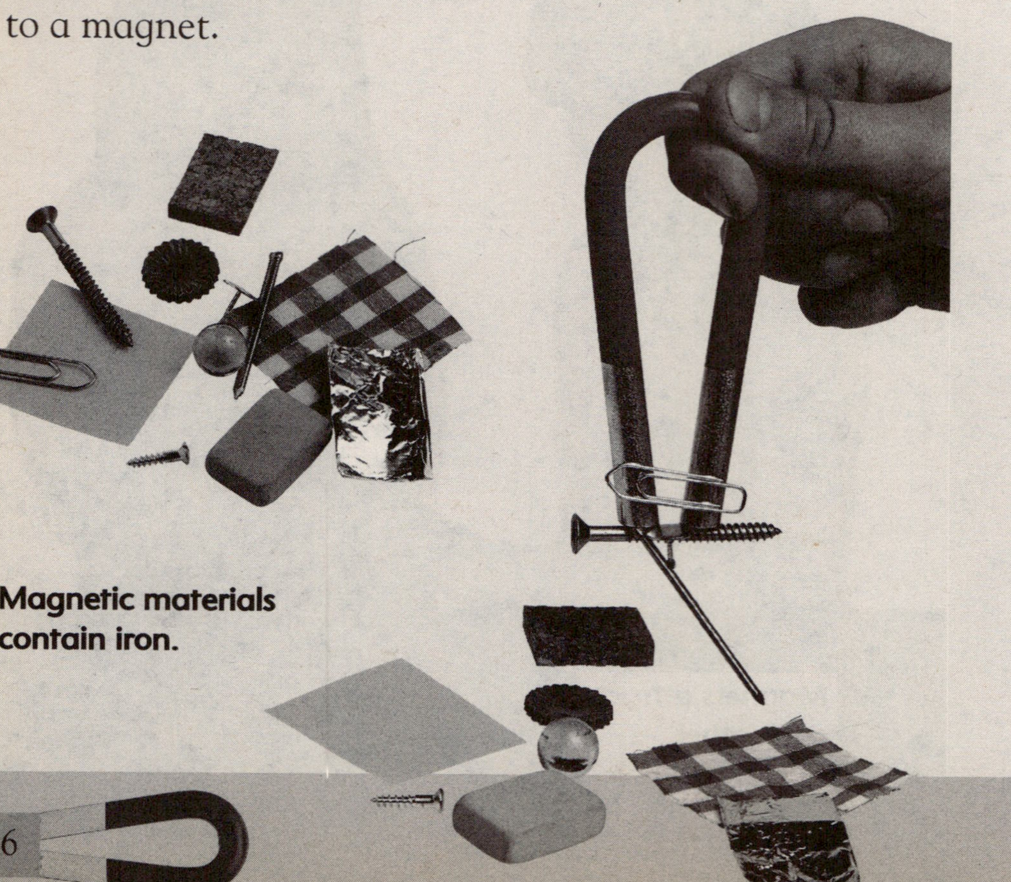

In this picture, metal balls are attracted to a magnet. Some of the balls do not touch the magnet. They stick to other balls. This is because the balls have become part of a magnetic field.

A magnetic field is the area of magnetism around a magnet. Objects in a magnetic field act like magnets. You can take a chain of balls away from the real magnet. The balls behave like magnets for a while. Then they slowly lose their magnetism.

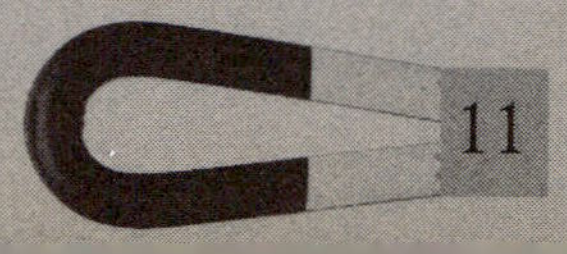

Making Magnets

If you have one magnet, you can make another magnet.

To do this, you need something made from magnetic material, such as a nail, a spoon, or a metal rod. Rub a magnet across the object about thirty times in one direction. You will create magnetism that was not there before. Your new magnet will attract or repel other magnetic materials.

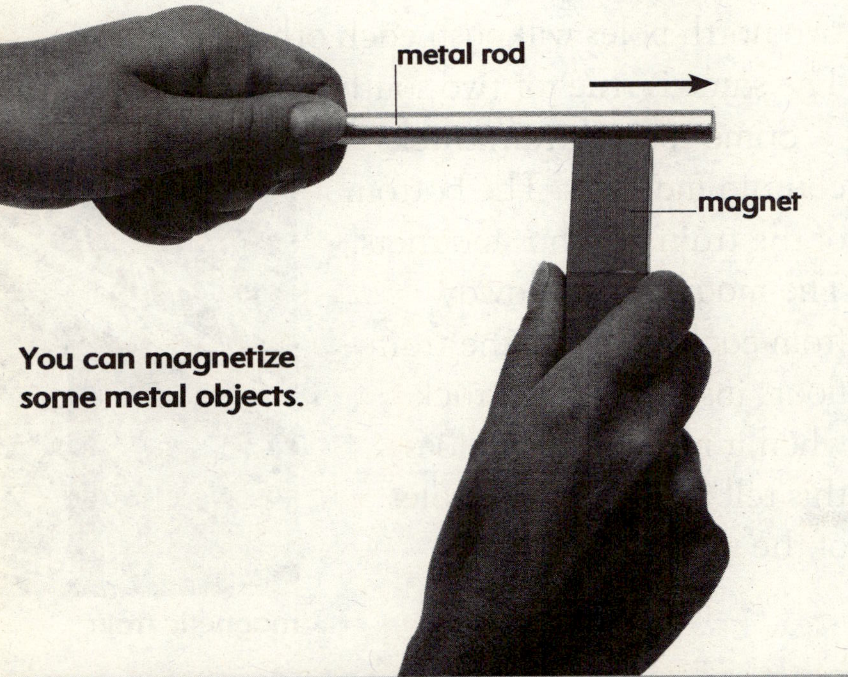

You can magnetize some metal objects.

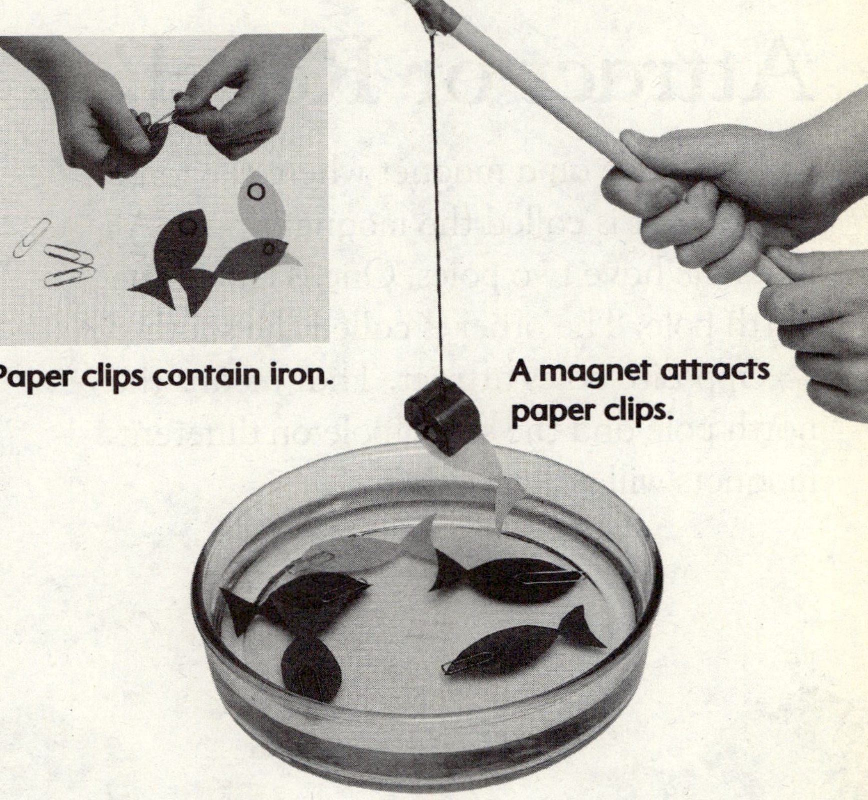

Paper clips contain iron.

A magnet attracts paper clips.

You can use magnets to make a game.

Cut some fish shapes from colored plastic or from a milk carton. Slip a paper clip onto each fish. Make a magnetic fishing pole by tying a magnet onto a string.

Drop your fish into a bowl of water and go fishing!

Take turns with a friend until all the fish are caught. Can you catch many fish at once?

Attract or Repel?

The place on a magnet where the force is strongest is called the magnet's pole. All magnets have two poles. One is called the north pole. The other is called the south pole.

Opposite poles attract. That means the north pole and the south pole on different magnets will pull together.

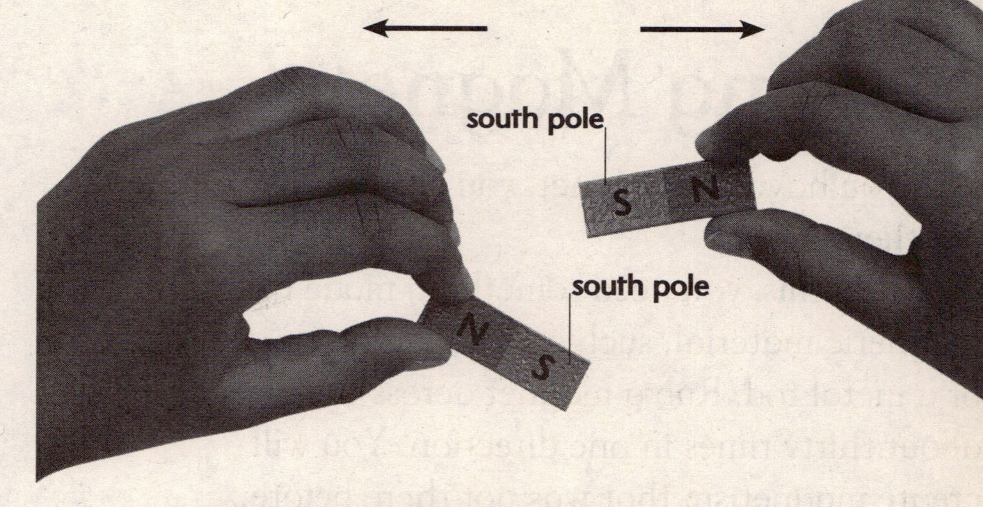

Poles that are alike repel.

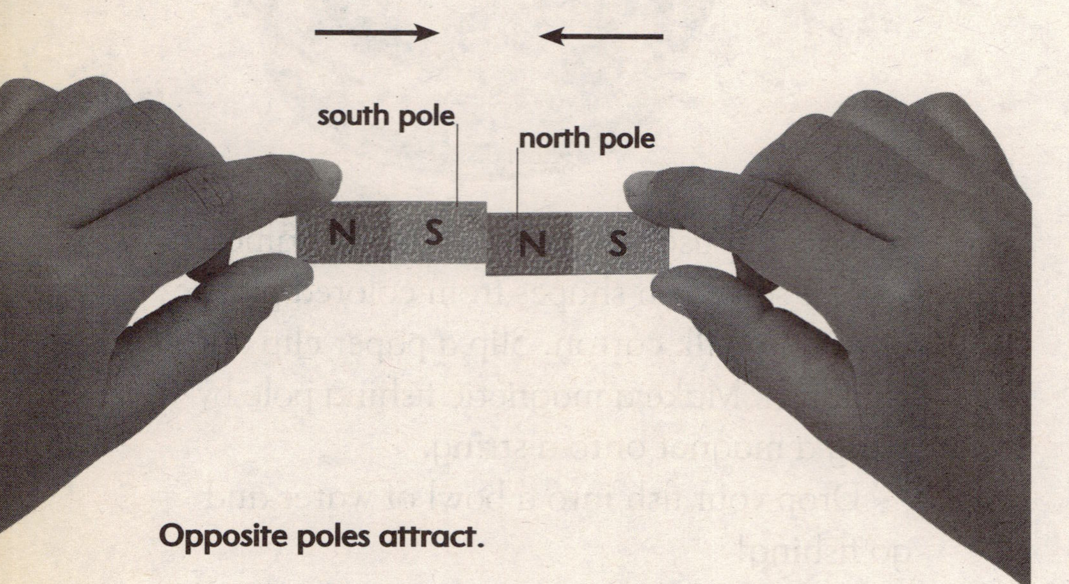

Opposite poles attract.

Poles that are alike repel. That means that two north poles will push each other away. The same is true for two south poles.

Some special train tracks contain magnets. The bottom of the train also has magnets. The magnets push away from each other, so the train floats just above the track when it moves. What does this tell you about the poles of the magnets?

magnetic train

Science

How Sound Travels

by Kim Borland

Genre	Comprehension Skill	Text Features	Science Content
Nonfiction	Important Details	• Captions • Labels • Table • Glossary	Sound

Scott Foresman Science 2.11

PEARSON
Scott Foresman

DK

ISBN 0-328-13801-0

90000

9 780328 138012

scottforesman.com

Vocabulary	Extended Vocabulary
loudness	decibels
pitch	echoes
vibrate	echolocation
	frequency
	sound waves

What did you learn?

1. Why might you hear thunder after you see a flash of lightning?

2. What are sound waves?

3. **Writing** in Science Many bats use echolocation to find their way around and to catch moths in the dark. Write to explain how bats do this. Use words from the book as you write.

4. **Important Details** In your own words tell some important details you've learned about the three main parts of the ear and how they work.

Picture Credits
Every effort has been made to secure permission and provide appropriate credit for photographic material. The publisher deeply regrets any omission and pledges to correct errors called to its attention in subsequent editions.

Photo locators denoted as follows: Top (T), Center (C), Bottom (B), Left (L), Right (R), Background (Bkgd).

7 Rob Matheson/Corbis; 9 (T) ©Royalty-Free/Corbis;13 David R. Frazier Photolibrary, Inc./Alamy Images; 14 Jonathan Blair/Corbis; 19 Oliver Benn/Getty Images; 23 Bill Ross/Corbis.

Scott Foresman/Dorling Kindersley would also like to thank: 11 (CA) Dennoyer-Geppert Intl/DK Images.

Unless otherwise acknowledged, all photographs are the copyright © of Dorling Kindersley, a division of Pearson.

ISBN: 0-328-13801-0

Copyright © Pearson Education, Inc.

Glossary

decibels	units used to measure the loudness of sound
echoes	sound waves bouncing off solid objects
echolocation	using bouncing sound waves to locate objects
frequency	the number of sound waves per second
sound waves	vibrations made by sound

How Sound Travels

by Kim Borland

What You Already Know

Sounds are all around! Sound is made when an object vibrates.

There are different ways to describe sound. One way is by its loudness. Some sounds are soft. Some are loud.

Another way to describe sound is by its pitch. Objects that vibrate quickly make a sound with a high pitch. Some birds can make high-pitched sounds. Objects that vibrate slowly make a sound with a low pitch. Bullfrogs can make low-pitched sounds.

Sound moves through solids, liquids, and gases. Sound travels fast through gases. Sound travels even faster through liquids. Sound travels fastest through solids.

bullfrog

Sounds Good!

We live in a world full of sounds! Some are soft, and some are loud. Some are high-pitched, and some are low-pitched.

Almost everything you do makes a sound. The next time you shake a box of cereal, listen to the sounds. The next time you shout to a friend across the playground, listen to the sounds. The next time you watch fireworks, listen to the sounds. When you turn the last page of this book, listen to the sounds.

How many different sounds do you think you hear in just one day? You'd probably be amazed to know!

Animals use their bodies to make sounds. A cricket rubs its wings together. A rattlesnake shakes the rattle in its tail. A lobster rubs its antenna along the side of its head.

Now that you know what sound is and how it is made, read on to find out more about how sound travels.

What kinds of sounds do fireworks make?

Sound Waves

Every sound you hear is caused by very fast movements, or vibrations. When an object vibrates, the air around it begins to vibrate too. The vibrations spread out like waves. They are called sound waves. When the sound waves reach our ears we hear the sound.

When you tap a tuning fork, it will vibrate and make sound waves. The sound waves will travel to your ear.

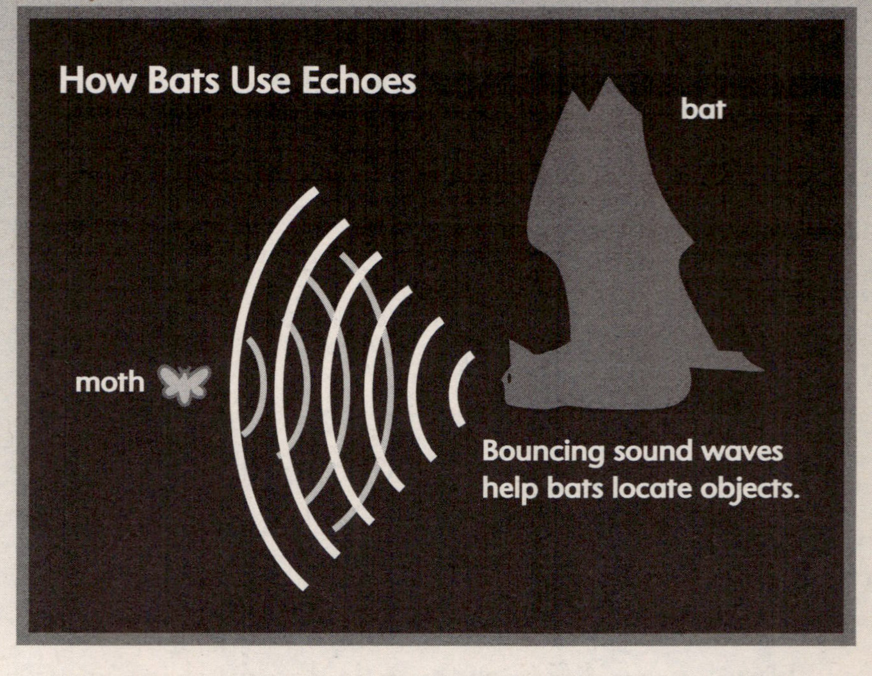

Bats also use echolocation to hunt. When a bat sends out a high-pitched sound, the sound waves may reach a moth. The sound waves bounce, or echo, off the moth. They return to the bat. Now the bat knows where the moth is and can catch it.

Scientists use a kind of echolocation, called sonar, to locate objects under the water. Scientists bounce sound waves off the ocean floor so they can tell how deep the water is. Sonar can help scientists find schools of fish and sunken ships.

Using Echoes

Some animals use echoes to find their way around and to hunt for food. Most bats sleep during the day and hunt for food at night. They fly around in total darkness. They cannot see where they are going.

As they fly, some bats make short, high-pitched sounds. The waves bounce off objects all around them. The echoes tell the bats where the objects are. This is called echolocation. Echolocation keeps bats from crashing into things.

Bats use echolocation
to hunt.

If you touch a
vibrating tuning fork
to water, the sound
waves will make
the water move.

Sound waves can travel in all directions. Sound waves vibrate at different speeds. Sound waves are invisible but if you could see them, they would look a little like small waves, or ripples. If you drop a pebble into a bowl of water, you can see ripples spreading out all around. Sound waves spread out all around too.

Sound waves move
like water ripples.

Speed of Sound

Which do you think travels faster, sound or light?

Have you ever watched a thunderstorm? Did you hear the thunder? Did you see the lightning? Which came first?

Thunder and lightning happen at the same time but during a thunderstorm you may see lightning before you hear the sound it makes.

You can see lightning as soon as it happens because light travels so fast. You don't hear the thunder until a few seconds later. That's because sound travels more slowly than light.

Next time you are in a thunderstorm, count the seconds between seeing the lightning and hearing the thunder.

Some places, such as theaters and concert halls, are built in special ways. People want the sound waves to travel and reach everyone in the room, but too many bouncing echoes would ruin a performance or music concert.

People build theaters and concert halls so they have special shapes. They use special materials to cover the walls, ceilings, and floors. All this is done to make sure the sound waves travel just right.

140

Bouncing Sound

Sound waves can bounce. As sound waves move, they bump into different objects. When sound waves hit soft objects, the waves are soaked up like water soaking into a sponge. When sound waves hit hard objects, they bounce. Sound waves that bounce are called echoes.

You hear echoes in some places with high walls and ceilings, such as a school gym. Sound waves bounce off the walls and the ceiling many times.

The sound waves from the ringing clock bounce off the cardboard and travel to the boy's ears.

Sound and Matter

Sound waves can travel through a gas, such as air. They can travel though a liquid, such as water. Sound waves can even travel through solids.

Sound waves travel better through liquids and solids than through gases. The particles of liquids and solids are close together. The sound vibrations can jump fast from particle to particle.

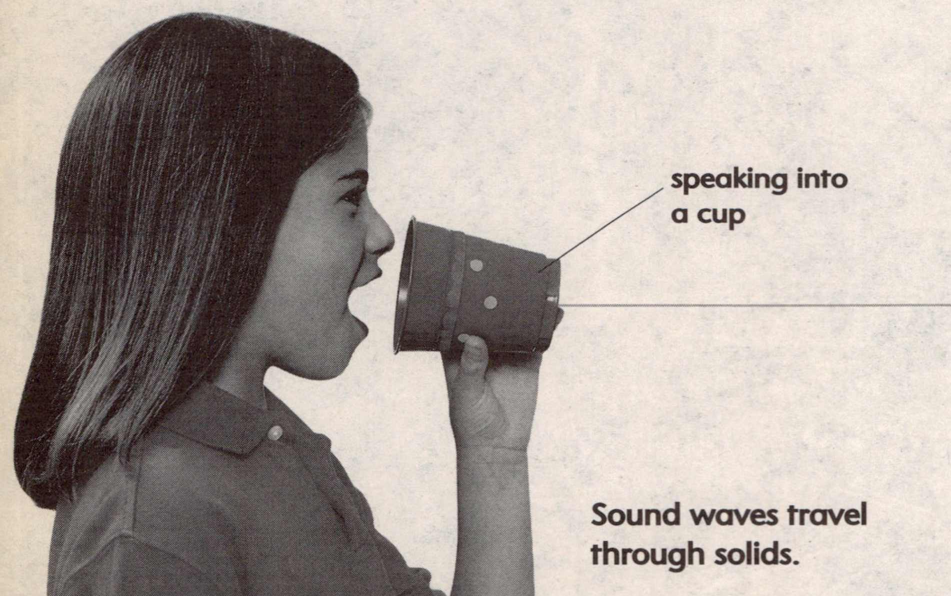

Sound waves travel through solids.

Changing Pitch

Fast-moving sounds can change pitch. The siren on a police car or an ambulance changes pitch as it passes. Next time you hear a siren listen carefully.

The sound of the siren starts out high-pitched. Then, when it is moving away, it changes to a lower pitch. How does this happen?

As it comes toward you, the sound waves the siren makes are squeezed together in front of the ambulance. They have a high frequency and make a high-pitched sound. When the ambulance has passed by, the opposite happens. The sound waves stretch out behind it. They have a lower frequency and make a low-pitched sound.

The pitch of an ambulance's siren can tell you how close it is.

There are some sounds that human ears cannot hear at all. Some sounds are too high-pitched or too low-pitched. Some animals can hear these sounds. Dogs can hear very high-pitched sounds. Pigeons can hear very low-pitched sounds.

pigeon

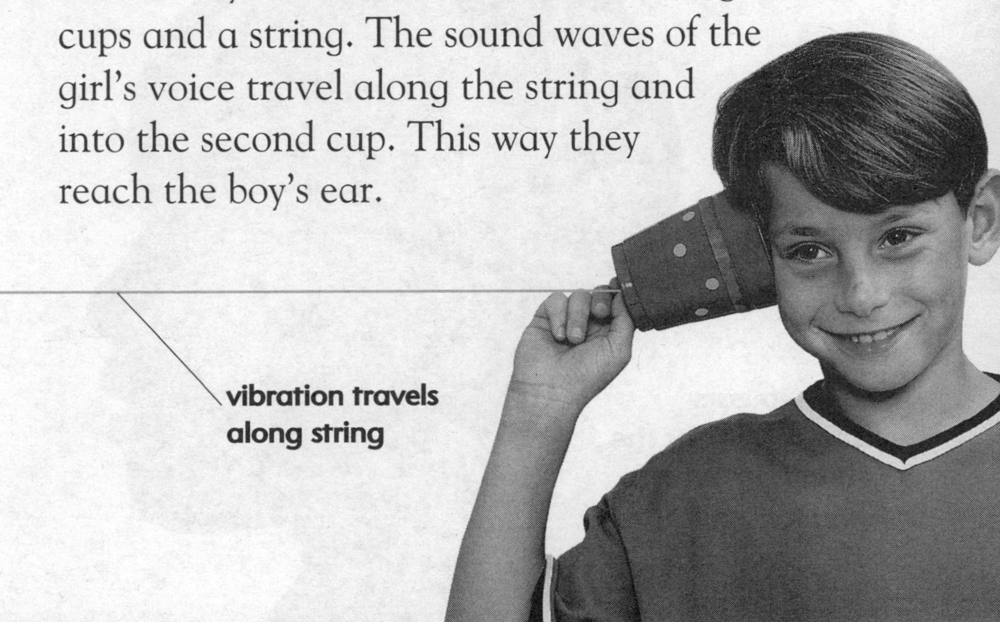

Sound travels best through solid objects. That's why these children can talk using two cups and a string. The sound waves of the girl's voice travel along the string and into the second cup. This way they reach the boy's ear.

How We Hear

We hear sounds with our ears. Our ears have three main parts: the outer ear, the middle ear, and the inner ear.

You can see part of your outer ear. The outer ear collects sound waves. The sound waves strike against the eardrum. They make the eardrum vibrate. It sends the sound waves to the middle ear.

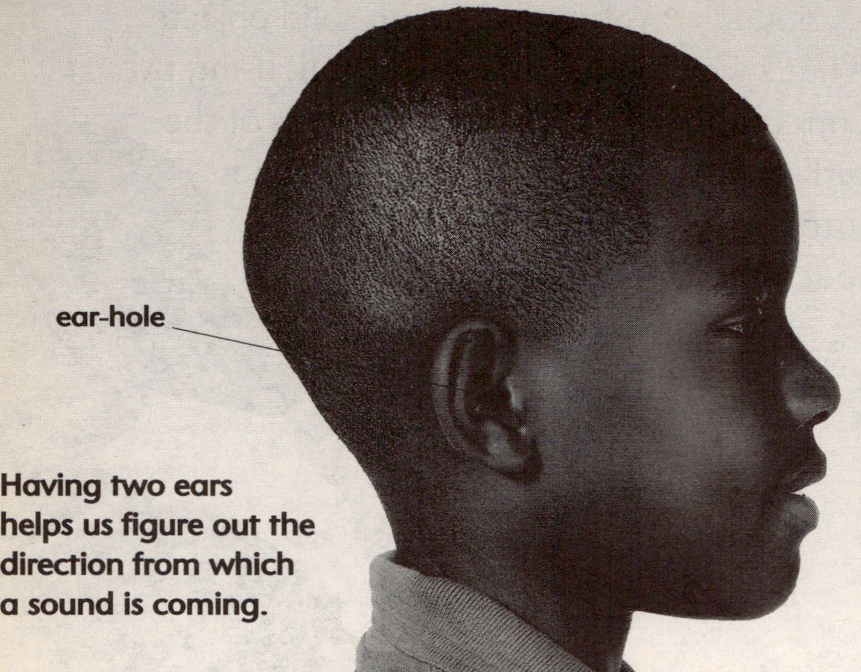

Having two ears helps us figure out the direction from which a sound is coming.

High or Low?

Every sound has a frequency. Frequency is the number of vibrations in one second. High-pitched sounds have a high frequency. Low-pitched sounds have a low frequency.

A whistle makes a high-pitched sound. The sound vibrations are very fast. A bullfrog makes a low-pitched sound. The sound vibrations are slow.

Human ears can hear some frequencies well, but very high-pitched and very low-pitched sounds are harder to hear.

You can hear different frequencies if you blow over the tops of bottles filled with different amounts of water.

Dangerous Sounds

Very loud sounds can be dangerous. Sounds of 120 decibels or more can be painful. They can damage your ears.

People who work in noisy places need to protect their ears from loud sounds. The sounds can harm their hearing.

In mountain areas, loud sounds can make snow come crashing down the mountain. This is called an avalanche. Avalanches can be dangerous.

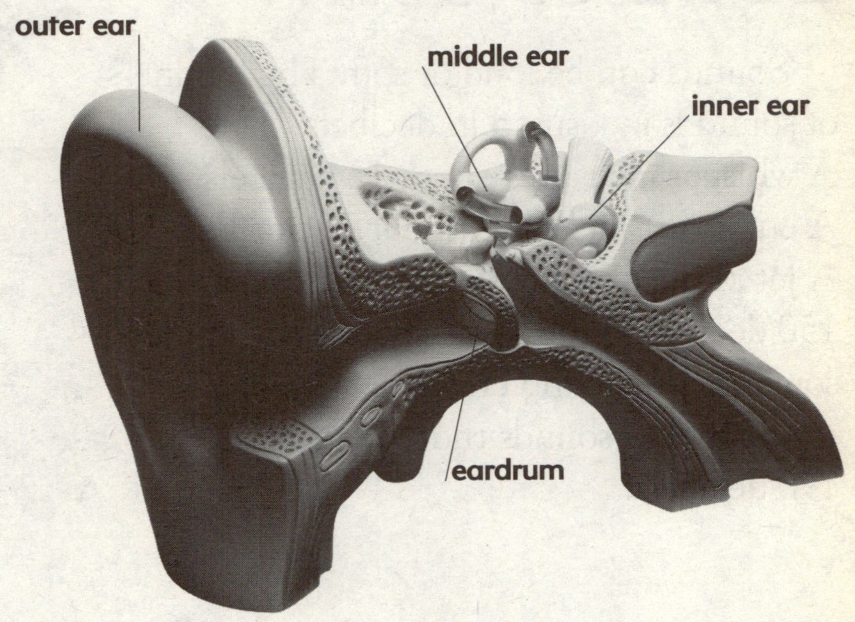

This worker is using a jackhammer. He wears special earmuffs to protect his ears from the loud sound.

The middle ear has three tiny bones. The vibrating eardrum moves these tiny bones. The bones pass the vibrations to the inner ear.

The inner ear is filled with a liquid. The vibrations make ripples in the liquid. Cells in the inner ear feel the ripples and change them into signals. These signals go to the brain. The brain lets us hear the signals as sound.

Loud or Soft?

Sounds can be loud or soft. The loudness of sound is measured in decibels (dB). A whisper measures about 12 decibels. A cat's purr measures about 25 decibels. A jet plane at takeoff measures about 150 decibels. Blue whales make the loudest sound of any living creature. The blue whale makes sounds that measure up to 190 decibels!

Jet planes are very loud at takeoff.

Have you ever cupped your hand behind your ear so you could hear better? When you do this you catch more sound waves. Your hand traps more waves and feeds them into your ear. The extra waves make the eardrum vibrate more strongly. You will hear the sound louder.

Soft to Loud Sounds

1 dB	leaves falling
25 dB	cat's purr
60 dB	people talking
150 dB	jet plane taking off
190 dB	call of the blue whale

Falling leaves are almost silent.

Guide to the Constellations

by Susan Jones Leeming

Genre	Comprehension Skill	Text Features	Science Content
Nonfiction	Alike and Different	• Captions • Labels • Glossary	Earth and Space

Scott Foresman Science 2.12

PEARSON

Scott Foresman

scottforesman.com

ISBN 0-328-13804-5

<table>
<tr><td>

Vocabulary

axis
constellation
crater
orbit
phase
rotation
solar system

</td><td>

Extended Vocabulary

ancient
hemisphere
planisphere
scale
stargazing
zodiac

</td></tr>
</table>

What did you learn?

1. How many zodiac constellations are there?

2. What kind of animal is the constellation Cancer?

3. **Writing** in Science In this book you read about lots of different constellations. Choose your favorite constellation. Write a paragraph to explain what you learned about that constellation and why it is your favorite. Use evidence from the text.

4. **Alike and Different** How are the zodiac constellations different from the other seventy-six constellations? How are they alike?

Picture Credits
Every effort has been made to secure permission and provide appropriate credit for photographic material. The publisher deeply regrets any omission and pledges to correct errors called to its attention in subsequent editions.

Photo locators denoted as follows: Top (T), Center (C), Bottom (B), Left (L), Right (R), Background (Bkgd).

Opener: L. Dodd /Photo Researchers, Inc.; 1 Jerry Lodriguss /Photo Researchers, Inc.; 3 (T) Getty Images; 4 John Chumack /Photo Researchers,Inc.; 11 (CR) J. Sanford /Photo Researchers, Inc.; 12 (BR) Eckhard Slawik / Photo Researchers, Inc.; 19 (CR) L. Dodd /Photo Researchers, Inc.; 20 (BR) NASA Headquarters - Greatest Images of NASA (NASA-HQ-GRIN)/NASA Image Exchange; 23 John Chumack /Photo Researchers, Inc.

Unless otherwise acknowledged, all photographs are the copyright © of Dorling Kindersley, a division of Pearson.

ISBN: 0-328-13804-5

Copyright © Pearson Education, Inc.

Guide to the Constellations

by Susan Jones Leeming

Glossary

ancient	old, from the distant past
hemisphere	the top or bottom half of Earth
planisphere	a map of the stars
scale	a tool used to measure weight
stargazing	looking at and studying the stars
zodiac	the name for 12 constellations that can be seen from both the Northern and Southern Hemispheres

Our Sun is really a star. It is the star that is closest to Earth. That is why it seems so big and so bright. All living things on Earth depend on the Sun's heat and light.

Earth spins on its axis, an imaginary line through its center. Earth rotates, or spins around completely, once a day. This rotation makes night and day. When the part of Earth where you live faces the Sun, you have day. When it rotates away from the Sun, you have night.

Earth is tilted on its axis and moves around the Sun in an orbit. Earth takes one year to orbit the Sun. Earth's tilt and its orbit around the Sun causes the seasons.

The Moon moves in an orbit around Earth. It takes about four weeks. The Moon goes through different phases, or shapes, during its orbit. The Moon has craters, which were caused by huge rocks crashing into it.

Do you see the Big Dipper or another picture in these stars?

What We Can See

Thousands of stars are visible in the sky. Over time people have seen many different pictures and shapes in these stars. All over the world people have used the stars to tell stories.

You too can make pictures with the stars in the night sky. You can make up your own stories, or you can look for the constellations you learned about. The next time you are outside at night, try stargazing!

Ursa Major

Another animal Orion hunted is Ursa Major, the Great Bear. Ancient Greeks saw two bears in the sky, Ursa Major and Ursa Minor. Ursa Major is the big bear. Ursa Minor is the small bear.

Seven stars of Ursa Major make up another constellation called the Big Dipper. A dipper is a deep spoon or a ladle. Can you see the handle of the Big Dipper starting at Ursa Major's tail? Some people see the Big Dipper as a wagon, a plow, or warriors. What do you see?

the Great Bear

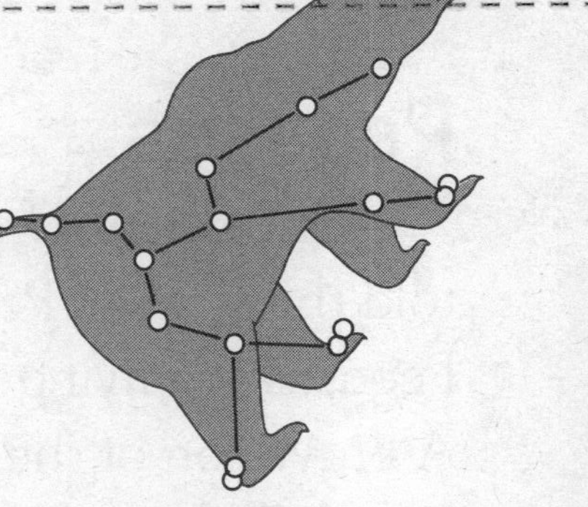

Big Dipper

Ursa Major

The Earth and the Moon are just two bodies in our solar system. There are eight other planets, most of which have moons as well. They all rotate around the Sun, making up our solar system.

The hundreds of stars that you see far away in the night sky are suns too. People have always looked at these stars and imagined lines connecting them, making pictures. These pictures are called constellations.

3

Stories of the Ancients

Ancient people looked up at the night sky and saw pictures. They imagined lines connecting the stars, making shapes called constellations. They gave these constellations names and told stories about them. The stories were about strange animals, heroes, and adventures. These stories were passed down to us.

Pegasus

The ancient Greeks told the story of Pegasus. Pegasus is a flying horse. A brave son of the god Zeus killed a monster. Pegasus flew out of the monster's neck. Even though the monster had been ugly and horrible, Pegasus was beautiful and good. Zeus, the king of all Greek gods, asked Pegasus to carry his lightning bolts.

Can you see the shape of a horse in the stars below? He is upside down! Can you imagine him running across the sky? What other pictures can you make with the stars of Pegasus?

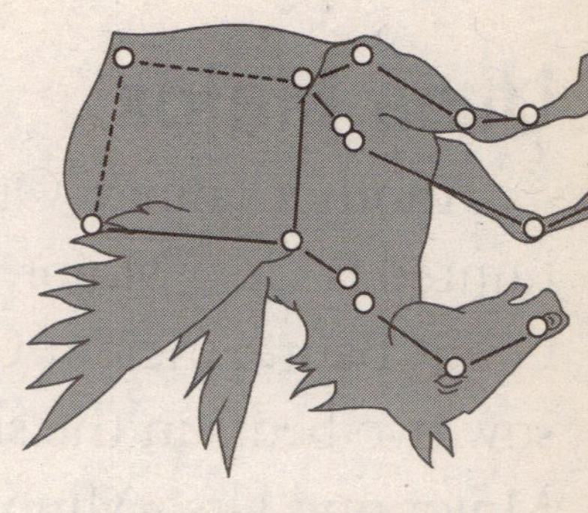
the Winged Horse

Pegasus

Orion

The constellation Orion was
seen by many ancient people.
Greeks, Romans, and Arabs all
have stories about this hunter. He
hunted animals like Taurus, the bull,
and Lepus, the rabbit, with his dogs.
Orion's life ended when he stepped
on a scorpion. The gods put Orion
in the sky with his dogs and many
animals to hunt. They put the
scorpion far away from him!

the Hunter

Orion

We can still see the pictures the ancients
saw in the night sky. They are many, many
miles away from each other, and we know the
stars in constellations do not have lines
between them.

There are about eighty-eight constellations.
Some are made of many stars. Others are
made of only a few. Different constellations
appear in the skies of the Northern and the
Southern Hemispheres.

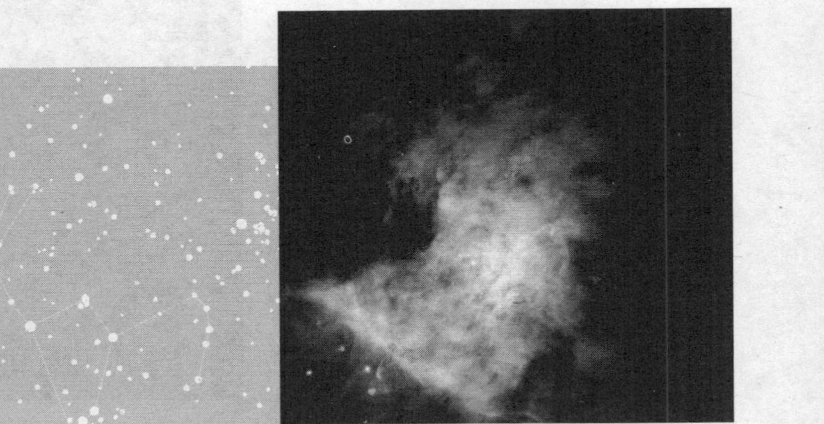
The star in the center of
Orion's sword is a nebula—
a huge gas formation
where stars are born.

Stargazing

You can look at the stars in the sky and study them using star maps. Some star maps are on a wheel. You can spin the wheel to the right place and season. This round star map is called a planisphere. Once you have found the correct location on the map, you are ready to begin stargazing.

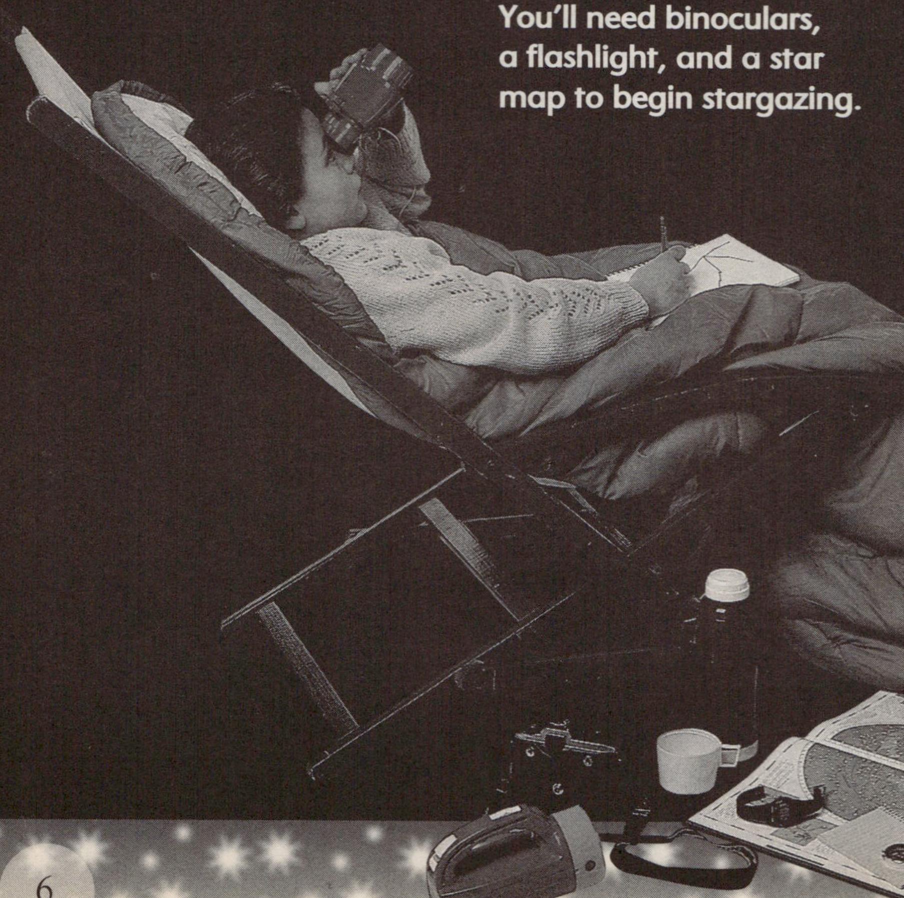

You'll need binoculars, a flashlight, and a star map to begin stargazing.

Crux

Crux is the Latin word for cross. The Crux constellation is also called the Southern Cross. This is because the Crux constellation is best seen from the Southern Hemisphere.

The stars that make up Crux are some of the brightest in the sky. Explorers have used Crux to help them sail across the sea. The bottom star points almost straight south.

the Southern Cross

Crux

Can you tell which star points south?

154

Canis Major

Canis means "dog" in Latin. Canis Major, or Greater Dog, was the dog of Orion, the brave hunter. Canis Minor, or Smaller Dog, was Canis Major's brother. Both dogs face other animal constellations in the sky. Canis Major faces Lepus, a rabbit-shaped constellation. Canis Minor faces Taurus, the bull. The ancient Greeks told stories about the two dogs chasing animals around the sky.

the Greater Dog

Canis Major

Ask a parent to take you to a place away from bright lights. Let your eyes get used to the darkness. Lie down and look up. Using a flashlight, compare what you see in the sky to what you see on your planisphere. Which constellations did you find? Which ones are still hiding from you?

Some star maps are printed on a wheel called a planisphere.

Zodiac Constellations

There are twelve constellations that can be seen from both the Northern and Southern Hemispheres. They are called the zodiac constellations. Each constellation appears in the night sky for about one month. Some people believe ancient farmers may have used the zodiac constellations as a calendar. When the spring constellations appeared, farmers knew it would soon be time to plant their crops. When the fall constellations appeared, they knew it was time to harvest.

People who lived thousands of years ago named the zodiac constellations. Different ancient people from around the world all told different stories about them. Some of the stories best known to us come from the ancient Greeks and Romans.

Cassiopeia

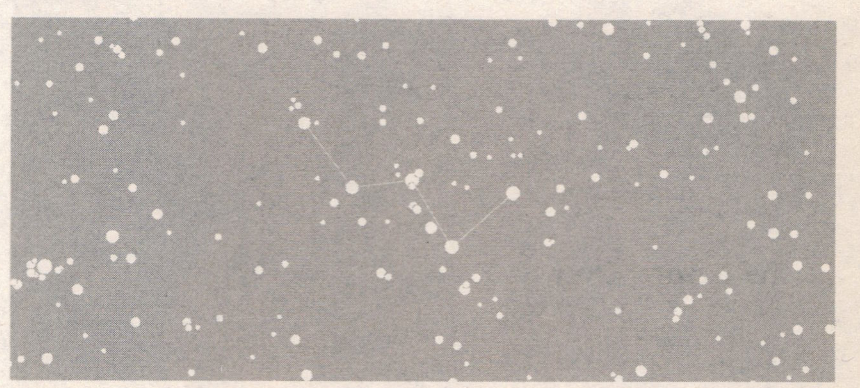
Cassiopeia

The W-shaped constellation is Cassiopeia. Cassiopeia and her husband, King Cepheus, were Andromeda's parents. Cassiopeia bragged that she and her daughter were more beautiful than the sea nymphs. Poseidon, the god of the sea, heard this and became angry. He sent floods to kill Cepheus's kingdom. King Cepheus asked a wise man for help. The wise man told Cepheus that if he let a sea monster eat Andromeda, then Poseidon would not flood their land. Cepheus was going to do this, but Perseus rescued Andromeda from death!

Cassiopeia

Other Constellations

There are many other constellations besides the twelve zodiac ones. Ancient people imagined stories about these other constellations too.

Andromeda

Andromeda was a beautiful Ethiopian princess. Perseus was a son of the god Zeus. He was on his way home from an adventure. He spotted beautiful Andromeda tied to a rock. A sea monster was about to eat her. Perseus killed the sea monster and saved the princess Andromeda. They fell in love and married each other.

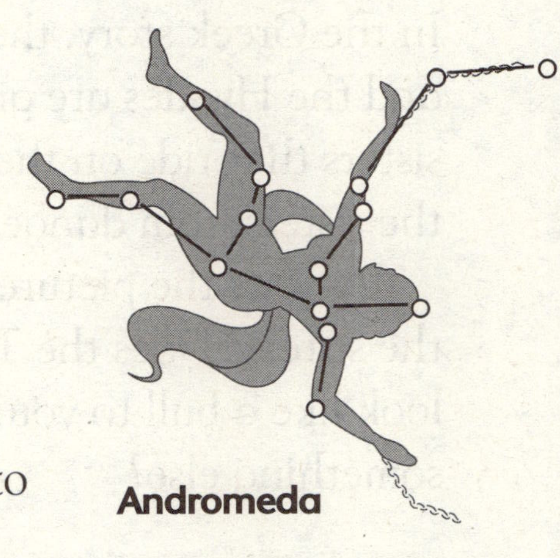

Andromeda

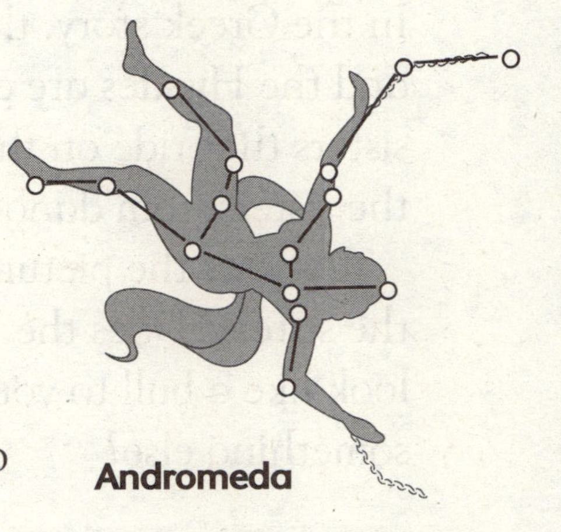

Andromeda

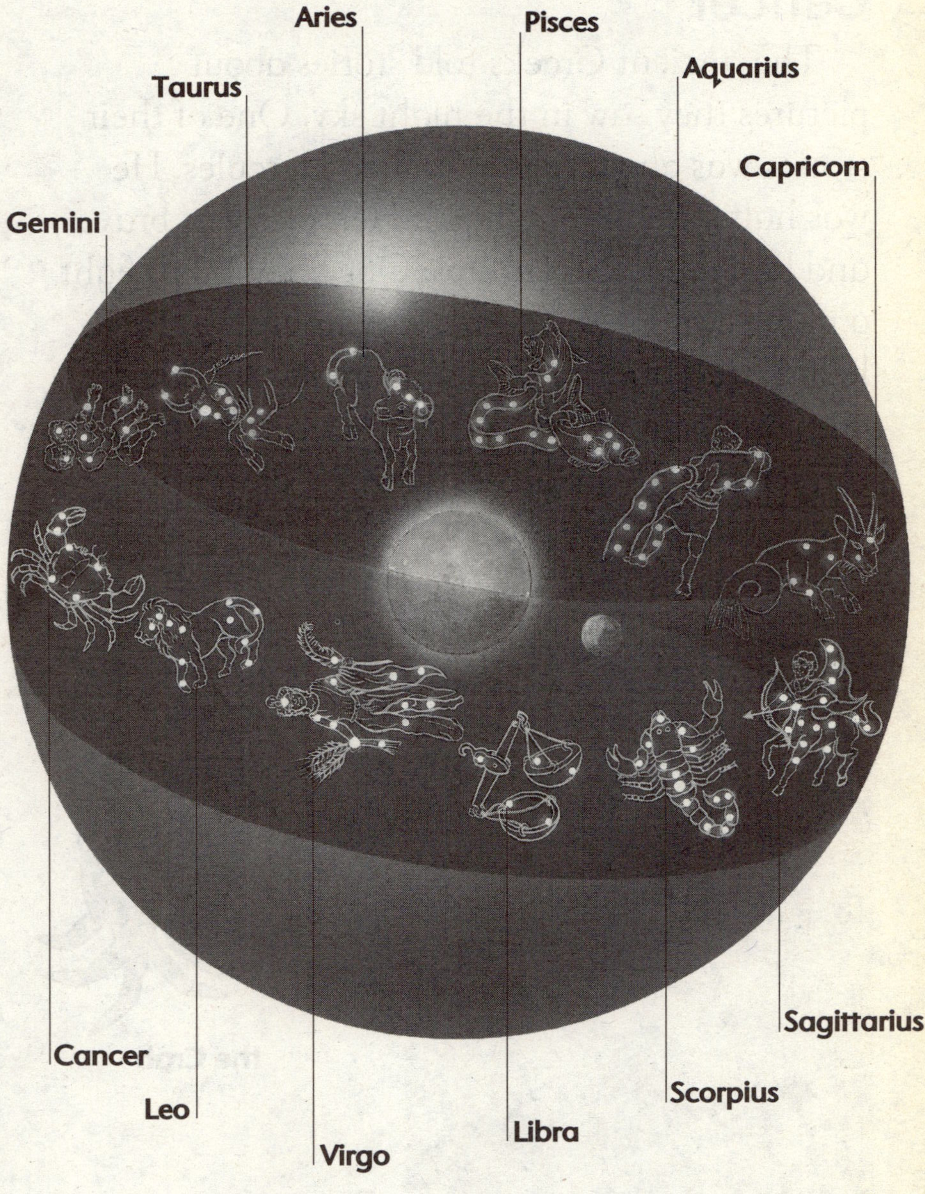

Cancer

The ancient Greeks told stories about pictures they saw in the night sky. One of their stories was about a hero named Hercules. He was half man and half god. Hercules was brave and had many adventures. Once he had to fight a monster named Hydra. A giant crab came to help Hydra fight Hercules. Hercules killed the crab and beat Hydra. Ancient Greeks named the six-star constellation after the crab. They called it Cancer.

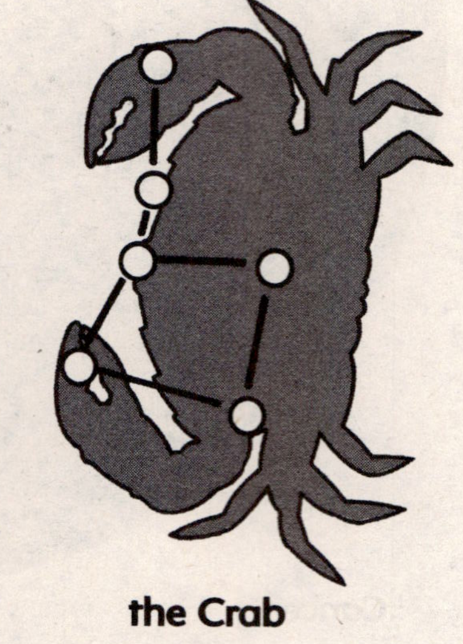
the Crab

Cancer

Taurus

The word Taurus means "bull" in Greek. The stars at the bull's back are named Pleiades. The stars at his nose are named Hyades. In the Greek story, the Pleiades and the Hyades are groups of sisters that ride on the bull. The bull protects the sisters from dangers in the sky.

Look at the picture below. Can you find the sisters? Does the Taurus constellation look like a bull to you? Can it look like something else?

the Bull

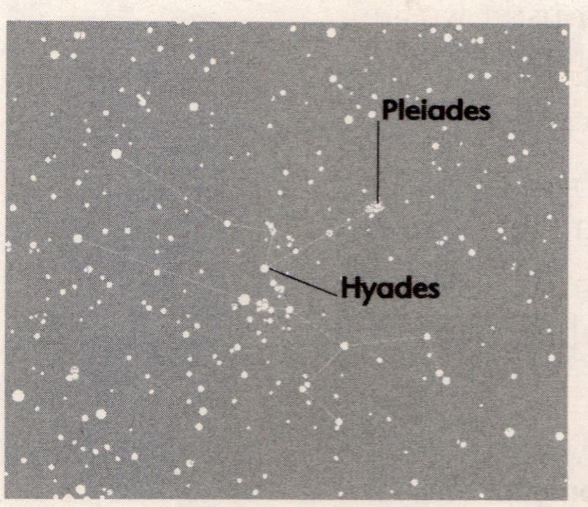

Taurus

Scorpius

Scorpions are dangerous animals. Their poison is stored in their tail. If a scorpion stings a person with its tail, the person could die.

The ancient Greeks did not see the scales in the stars of Libra. Instead they saw the claws of a scorpion. They named the constellation Scorpius. They told a story about the scorpion killing a brave hunter named Orion.

The people of Polynesia saw a fishing hook in the stars of Scorpius. Do you see Libra, a hook, or a scorpion in the picture below?

Scorpius

Gemini

The ancient Greeks told a story about the twins Castor and Pollux. Pollux was the son of the god Zeus. Castor was the son of a man and woman. One day Castor was killed. Pollux missed his brother very much. He asked his father, Zeus, if he could give Castor half of his long life. Zeus agreed. The brothers lived together again in the night sky.

Gemini

The two brightest stars in the Gemini constellation are named Castor and Pollux, the twin brothers.

Leo

Every summer the ancient Greeks saw a lion in the sky. They called this lion Leo. Remember Hercules, the hero? The gods gave Hercules twelve jobs. His first job was to kill a dangerous lion. Afterward, Hercules always wore the lion's fur on his back.

Can you see the picture of the lion in the stars below?

the Lion

Leo

The brightest star in Leo is Regulus.

Libra

Libra is the only zodiac constellation that is not a person or an animal. Libra is in the shape of scales. Scales are tools used for measuring weight. An object is placed on one side and weights are placed on the other side until the two sides balance. The weights are counted to find out how heavy the object is.

The ancient Romans told stories about Libra. The scales made them think of fairness or equality because a scale can show equal weights.

the Scales

Libra

Space and Technology

Flying Machines

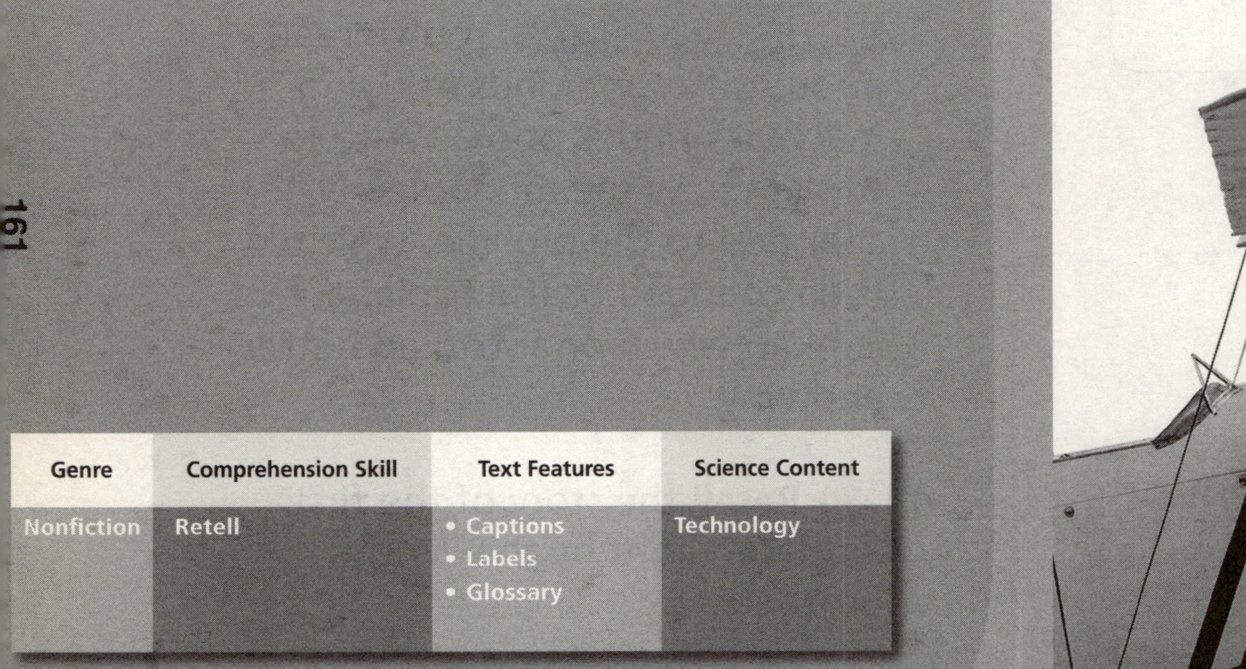

by Tess Mason

Genre	Comprehension Skill	Text Features	Science Content
Nonfiction	Retell	• Captions • Labels • Glossary	Technology

Scott Foresman Science 2.13

What did you learn?

1. What are two of the special tasks that helicopters are able to do? Why can they do these things?

2. Why do hot air balloons rise high into the air?

3. **Writing** in Science You've read about different kinds of flying machines in this book. Write to explain how the monoplane changed to the biplane, which then changed to the triplane. Explain which one worked better and why.

4. **Retell** the story of the first airplane flight by the Wright brothers.

Vocabulary	Extended Vocabulary
engine	aviators
invent	gasoline
manufacture	helicopter
meteorologist	helium
satellite	propane
technology	runway
transportation	
vaccine	

Picture Credits
Every effort has been made to secure permission and provide appropriate credit for photographic material. The publisher deeply regrets any omission and pledges to correct errors called to its attention in subsequent editions.

Photo locators denoted as follows: Top (T), Center (C), Bottom (B), Left (L), Right (R), Background (Bkgd).

1 (B) Bob Burch/Index Stock Imagery; 3 Age Fotostock; 6 (BL) Getty Images; 7 Gamma/Katz Pictures Limited; 8 (B) Bob Burch/Index Stock Imagery; 9 Bettmann/Corbis; 14 (B) Age Fotostock; 15 Gamma/Katz Pictures Limited.

Unless otherwise acknowledged, all photographs are the copyright © of Dorling Kindersley, a division of Pearson.

ISBN: 0-328-13807-X

Glossary

aviators	people who fly aircraft and study flying
gasoline	a common fuel
helicopter	an aircraft without wings that moves with propellers
helium	a very light gas
propane	a kind of gas used as fuel
runway	a paved strip of ground on which planes land and take off

Flying Machines

by Tess Mason

We use technology each day without even noticing it. Technology means using science to help us solve problems. People think up, or invent, ways to use science and technology.

New inventions change the way people live. One thing that has changed is the way we get from place to place. This is transportation. At one time we could only walk. Now we drive cars and fly planes. These kinds of transportation have engines. An engine is a machine that does work.

Another invention that has changed how we live is the vaccine. A vaccine is medicine that can help prevent disease. Doctors use technology in other ways too.

Transportation enables people to travel long distances.

Future Flights

From kites to the first airplane, flying machines have come a long way. Now we have helicopters and jet planes. We even have space shuttles that fly into outer space. People keep inventing new ideas for ways to fly. Maybe someday we'll be able to fly without planes. Who knows what we can do next? The sky is the limit!

Is this the future of flying?

Helicopters

The first useful helicopter was made in 1936 by Heinrich Focke and Gerd Achgelis. Helicopters are used for many things. They are small and fast to turn. Helicopters can hover. This means they can stay in the air without moving. They can also land without a runway. Helicopters are used for rescuing people. They are also used for observing animals in the wild.

an early helicopter

a modern helicopter

helicopter

Technology also helps people communicate, have fun, and work. A meteorologist studies the weather with information from satellites. A satellite is an object that revolves around a larger object. Satellites in space send pictures back to Earth. Meteorologists look at the pictures and tell us about the weather.

Technology is manufactured, or made. Sometimes technology is manufactured by people or sometimes machines do the work.

One of the most important technologies ever invented and manufactured is the flying machine. Flying machines have changed transportation. Today they are an important part of everyday life.

Up, Up, and Away

Have you ever been on a plane? What about a helicopter? Maybe you have dreamed of flying to the Moon. One hundred years ago planes were just a dream. Now we can get on an airplane and fly anywhere in the world. It took people thousands of years to get to this point.

For centuries, people have looked at birds fly through the skies, wishing they could do the same. People in China even tried to fly on kites three thousand years ago.

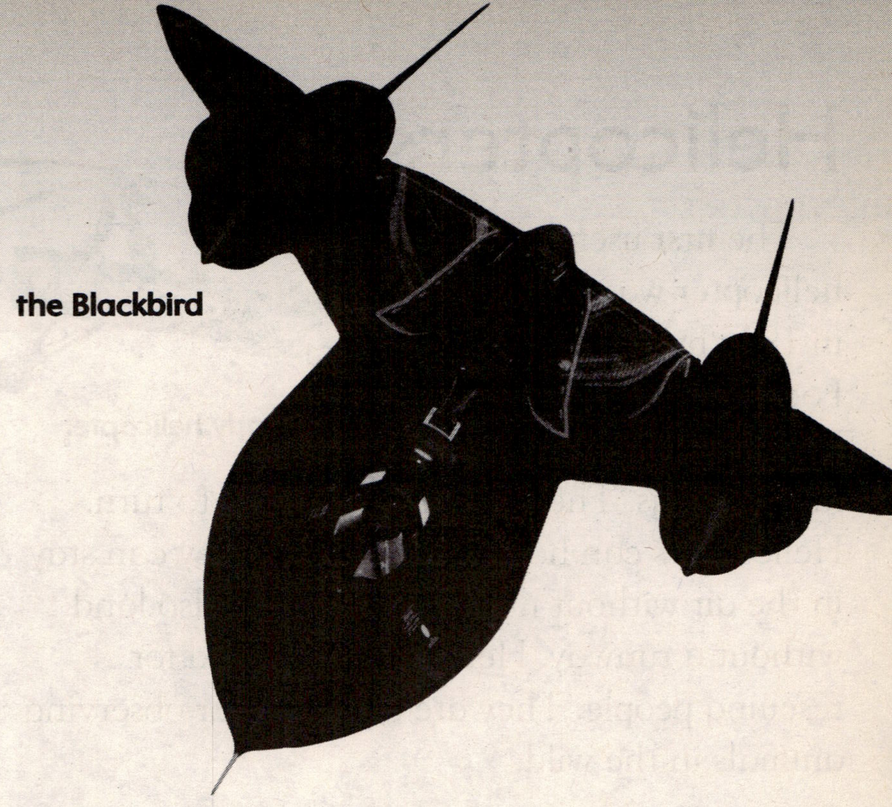
the Blackbird

Humans have dreamed of flying like birds for centuries.

modern propeller plane

Soon people started using airplanes for work. The U.S. Postal Service flew its first cross-country mail service in 1920. By 1924 it started a regular airmail service between New York and San Francisco. Planes carried mail much faster than trains had done.

The military has invented some of the fastest planes. The SR-71 "Blackbird" flew from New York to London in less than two hours! A regular plane takes about six hours to make this trip.

the Boeing 247

Airplanes became more and more important. In 1933 a company called Boeing flew the first modern passenger plane. It was called the 247. It carried ten passengers. More than thirty years later, in 1969, Boeing flew the "Jumbo Jet." The Jumbo Jet can carry more than four hundred passengers. It is still the largest airplane in the world.

Jumbo Jet

This steam-powered model was among the many experimental flying machines.

Leonardo da Vinci was a great artist and inventor. In the 1400s, he studied bird wings to make the first flying machines. For the next few hundred years, people tried many different ways to fly. The first airplane left the ground in 1903. Since then, we have learned a lot more about flight. Today there are many kinds of flying machines, such as planes, helicopters, and space shuttles.

Hot Air Balloons

One of the first flying machines was the hot air balloon. Warm air is lighter than cool air. Warm air rises. Hot air balloons can rise up into the sky because they are filled with hot air.

In 1783 the Montgolfier brothers used this idea. They made the first successful hot air balloon. To heat the air, they burned straw and wool.

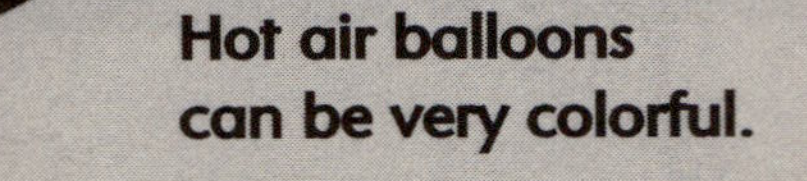

The Montgolfiers' balloon was the first-ever hot air balloon.

Hot air balloons can be very colorful.

Triplanes had three short wings. The pilot could steer better and see better.

The Wright brothers used a biplane design. Bi means "two." Biplanes have two pairs of wings. The monoplane could fly faster than the biplane, but the biplane was safer. It did not crash as often.

In World War I, triplanes were invented. Tri means "three." Triplanes had three pairs of wings. This made them easier to handle. Pilots could see better out of triplanes because the wings were shorter.

The success of the Wright brothers' first flight inspired inventors all around the world. Many people tried to build their own aircraft and came up with new ideas. In 1909 Elise Deroche became the first female pilot in the world. In the same year, Louis Blériot flew across the English Channel in his monoplane, the *Blériot XI*. Blériot designed the first successful monoplane. Mono means "one." Monoplanes have only one pair of wings.

Louis Blériot flew over the English Channel in his monoplane.

Biplanes have two pairs of wings.

These days hot air balloons use propane for fuel. The propane fires the engines that heat the air.

Hot air balloons are a great way to fly, but they are hard to steer. They are not easy to use for traveling. Even so, in 2002 Steve Fossett became the first man to fly a hot air balloon all the way around the world!

Steve Fossett became the first man to fly around the world in this hot air balloon, called *Spirit of Freedom*.

Airships

Henri Giffard built
the first airship.

Since hot air balloons
are so hard to steer, early
inventors kept searching
for a better flying machine.
In 1852 Henri Giffard flew
the first airship. The airship
uses gases that are lighter than air, such as
helium. This lets them rise up into the sky.
Airships have an engine so they can be more
easily steered. Today some airships can stay
up in the air for days.

a modern airship

Powered Flight

Aviators are people who fly aircraft and study
flying. Powered planes are planes that use
engines and fuel, such as gasoline, to fly.

Two aviators, called the Wright brothers,
made the first powered airplane flight. Their
plane was called the *Flyer*. It weighed
605 pounds. The flight only lasted 12 seconds!
The *Flyer* traveled 120 feet. The Wright brothers'
historic first flight led to today's airplanes.

The Wright brothers made the first powered flight in 1903.